More praise for *The Woman W*

"The Woman Who Watches O
altering episodes as [Hogan's]
up on a U.S. Army base in Ge
nation's—blighted history in Oklahoma, and the defining moment
when, as an adult in night school, 'the words came'—bringing with
them a 'light-bearing, soul-saving presence that illuminated my heart
and mind and altered my destiny.' "   —*Elle*

"A deeply courageous account of Hogan's personal and tribal history
. . . rich with stories that examine every aspect of the physical world,
looking for the metaphorical gem at its center."
                                              —Pam Houston, *O* magazine

"With threads of personal history, tribal memory and lore, Linda
Hogan has woven a blanket rich and complicated. Its color is hope,
its design healing."   —Greg Sarris, author of *Watermelon Nights*

"The Watcher over the world catalogues memory, spins the threads
into tangible patterns to illustrate places of danger, harbors for refuge.
Hogan's memoir is a piece of that immense undertaking. It reminds
us who we are, where we have been, where we are going."
                                 —Joy Harjo, author of *Map to the Next World*

"Linda Hogan's report of pain and injury comes to us from a deeply
disturbing place. She hands us a map that might be called the geography of hopelessness, but she has written 'forgive' and 'love' across
its tortured hills. Her bravery leaves us standing in silence."
                                                              —Barry Lopez

"The Woman Who Watches Over the World is a moving and haunt-
ingly clear-eyed personal and tribal history about the making of an
American conscience. Like her Indian mustang horse, Mystery,
Hogan is more than 'a beautiful survivor.' She is a compassionate witness who reminds us: 'When a person says, "I remember," all things
are possible.' "   — Brenda Peterson, author of *Build Me an Ark*

THE WOMAN WHO

WATCHES OVER THE WORLD

A NATIVE MEMOIR

▲

LINDA HOGAN

W. W. NORTON & COMPANY

NEW YORK / LONDON

For information about permission to reproduce selections
from this book, write to Permissions,
W. W. Norton & Company, Inc., 500 Fifth Avenue,
New York, NY 10110

Manufacturing by Quad/Graphics, Fairfield Inc.
Book design by JAM Design
Production manager: Leelo Märjamaa-Reintal

Library of Congress Cataloging-in-Publication Data

Hogan, Linda.
The woman who watches over the world : a native memoir / Linda Hogan.
p. cm.
ISBN 0-393-05018-1
1. Hogan, Linda. 2. Authors, American—20th century—Family relationships.
3. Authors, American—20th century—Biography.
4. Indians of North America—Biography.
5. Indian authors—Biography. 6. Indian women—Biography.
7. Hogan, Linda—Family. I. Title.

PS3558.O34726 Z47 2001
818'.5409—dc21

[B]   00-049005

ISBN 0-393-32305-6 pbk

W. W. Norton & Company, Inc., 500 Fifth Avenue, New York, N.Y. 10110
www.wwnorton.com

W. W. Norton & Company Ltd., Castle House,
75/76 Wells Street, London W1T 3QT

7 8 9 0

For my fine parents, for
Janya and Marie, my grandchildren,
and our growing love. And for
young Native women everywhere.

All over the earth faces of all living things are alike.

Mother Earth has turned these faces out of the earth with
tenderness.

—STANDING BEAR

A vast similitude interlocks all,

All spheres, grown, ungrown, small, large, suns,
moons, planets,

All distances of place however wide,

All distances of time, all inanimate forms . . .

All gaseous, watery, vegetable, mineral processes,
the fishes, the brutes . . .

—WALT WHITMAN, Leaves of Grass

I come from warriors
yet I can hardly speak.
That's why I write this.

CONTENTS

ACKNOWLEDGMENTS

FIRST OF ALL, I would like to express thanks to Georgianna Sanchez for so kindly permitting me to write about our day with her family. I am grateful to my loving parents, who saw me through more than just an accident. My cousin Sakej Youngblood Henderson has been generous with me in all ways these past few years, and I thank him. I thank the beautiful and growing next generation, Tanya Thunderhorse, for being such a loving part of my life. I send love and the hope of healing to my daughter Marie. I am happy there are still people in the world such as Lori and Ted Frost who are compassionate. I thank writer Connie Studer, my longtime friend, for helping me, in spite of her own health problems. I'm eternally grateful to my brother, photographer Larry Henderson, for his kindness to me, even at the expense of his own rest. I send thanks to my sister, Donna Porter, with whom I always laughed. I thank Marilyn Auer, my central friend over the years of our circling lives. Thank you, Marlene Blessing, for your earrings and many other gifts. I am indebted also to Sharon Brogan and the buffalo, as well as to Shari Curtis and her buffalo bone soup.

My neighbor Mary Helen, who helped me through brain injuries, broken bones, depression, and walkers, continues to be kind and supportive and a wonderful friend. So does neighbor Cheri Thomas. Gratitude also to Kay Miller and Denise Stoner for baby-sitting me a couple of days. Thanks to Patrick, who shared with me the heartbreak of a disintegrating family. And thanks always to my old, dear friends Becky and Joe Hogan. I'm extremely thankful to my agent, Beth Vesel, who was wonderful to me through very difficult times, and to her assistant, Emily. My thanks also to my editor, Jill Bialosky, for her insight into an earlier version of this book, and to her assistant, Drake Bennett. For Jean Fortier, I am grateful from the bottom of my feet to the top of my head for your kind guidance. I thank also, among many doctors, Dr. Ricardo Esparza, Dr. Gerber, Dr. Granston, Dr. Keatly, and Dr. Julie Stapleton, and numerous other medical professionals. I hope you remember who you are and forgive me for not listing all your names. And I thank my wonderful horse trainer, Liz Olde, who has been more than patient and who helps me to safety. I must express my love for my horses Kelli, the starved and wounded, and Mystery (Misty), the wild mustang who was rounded up, broken in the bones, and taken away from her land and herd; she is now a dream horse. I acknowledge my uncles Wesley and Jake, and the other horsemen in my family. This book is also for my grandchildren: Vivian and Michael, and Cammy, Danielle, and Michael, and to Kathy Griffith, who found me through my book *Solar Storms.* I am grateful to Barbara Kingsolver for her very kind support with my other books. Thank you, Pat and Jack Porter, my nephews, for helping me move even though I didn't want to. And thanks to the Dyer family and the little cabin with its healing trees, stones, mountain lions, and elk. I gratefully acknowledge both the Highland Rescue Team and the Idledale Fire and Rescue Team. You folks were great *and* fast. And above all, the person who has been here the most for me, the kindest woman I know with the largest heart, my coeditor on projects, my sometimes inspiration, my always most beloved friend and a woman with a beautiful soul, I thank sister writer Brenda Peterson.

GEOGRAPHY:
AN INTRODUCTION

AS AN INDIAN woman, I have always wondered why others want to enter our lives, to know the private landscape inside a human spirit, the map existing inside tribal thoughts and traditional knowledge. It is a search, I think, for a sense of meaning and relationship. Others seek us out to find answers to questions minds and bodies new to this continent haven't yet even asked. I want to speak to these silences because they rise up in this part of my life as if I can lay a human history out before me and hold a light to it, and in that light is the history of a continent as well. Self-telling is rare for a Native woman, but when I work on reservations with young people they want to know how I survived my life. I wish I could offer up a map and say, "This way." But it is not so easy. There are no roads through, no paths known, no maps or directions.

The cairns and markers have been taken away and broken. Who knows where to step, how to find wholeness? It's not that we have lost the old ways and intelligences, but that we are lost from them. They are always here, patient, waiting for our return to their beauty, their integrity, their reverence for life. Until we do, we will have restless spirits. So this, my human history within a larger one, perhaps will serve as something of a beginning.

Our stories began not just with our grandmothers, our ancestors, but maybe four million years ago in the dark matter of some distant edge of earth or corner of space. Who knows where we enter? There are theories, constantly changing; we are still a mystery. Mystery is part of each life, and maybe it is healthier to uphold it than to spend a lifetime in search of half-made answers.

Still, as humans, we want truth. We are searchers. Our stories, our courthouses, our lives, contemporary anxieties and depressions are all searches full with this desire. Humans want truth the way water desires to be sea level and moves across the continent for the greater ocean.

"Memory is a field full of psychological ruins," wrote French philosopher Gaston Bachelard. For some that may be true, but memory is also a field of healing that has the capacity to restore the world, not only for the one person who recollects, but for cultures as well. When a person says "I remember," all things are possible.

There are ways in, journeys to the center of a life, through time, through air, matter, dream, and thought. The ways in are not always mapped or charted, but sometimes being lost, if there is such a thing, is the sweetest place to be. And always, in this search, a person might find that she is already there, at the center of a world. It may be a broken world, but it is glorious nevertheless.

In my life, the wounds of history, illness, the split second of an accident, have turned me to the spirit in a search for healing, wherever it can be found. And in that turn is the fact of the body, not only in the world, but as a process of the world.

▲   ▲   ▲

WHEN PAIN TOOK up residence in my body, I spent years learning it, speaking with it, befriending it, dreaming and seeking out the medicines and plants that might heal it, trying to coax it away with charms, as with doctors of all kinds. Finally, my doctors became earth, water, light, and air. They were animals, plants, and kindred spirits. It wasn't healing I found or a life free from pain, but a kind of love and kinship with a similarly broken world.

We humans have always believed we had greater powers than we had. And with such little protection beneath our shelters of wood and shingle-thin roofs, the belief systems have failed us because belief alone does not save us in a world of matter. Yet we do have the power of our talking, our stories. Even so, all the elements of ourselves and our world are more than can be held in words alone; there is something else beyond our knowing.

This is a book about love. It didn't begin that way. I sat down to write about pain and wrote, instead, about healing, history, and survival. The work revealed to me that there is a geography of the human spirit, common to all peoples.

THE WOMAN WHO WATCHES
OVER THE WORLD

Broken

I REMEMBER THE first time I saw the clay woman. I was
with Georgianna Sanchez. We were in a museum gift shop.
The clay woman from San Martín, Mexico, was full and beautiful. Attached to earth, she flew over it. She wore a dress of
stars. Her black hair flowed behind her, and on her clay feet
were little black shoes. Beneath her, the earth was orange. It
would have looked somewhat like a pumpkin if not for the
dividing lines of countries, continents, and oceans. Her nose
was large, her breasts heavy and pointed, her stomach attached
to earth, just above North America. Her name was written on
a tag, "The Bruja Who Watches Over the Earth." *Bruja* is the
Spanish word for a woman healer, soothsayer, or sometimes a
witch.

▲   ▲   ▲

I LOVED THIS flying soothsayer who protected the lands
beneath her. She was connected to them by her very body, the

very same clay. Like nearly all first people, she was shaped from the planet to which she was connected.

I bought the clay woman and asked the clerk to mail her to me, then I returned home, anticipating the day The Woman Who Watches Over the World would appear.

When she arrived, she wasn't whole. Her legs were broken off, the gray interior clay exposed beneath the paint. I glued them back on. Then she began to fall apart in other ways. Her nose broke. Soon one of her hands fell off. The woman who watches over the world was broken. Despite my efforts, she remained that way, fragmented and unhealed. At first I was disappointed, but then I thought, Yes, the woman who watches over us is as broken as the land, as hurt as the flesh people. She is a true representation of the world she flies above. Something between us and earth has broken. That is what the soothsayer says.

▲   ▲   ▲

ONE DAY, A few years later, Georgianna and I sat together at the Pacific Ocean. There was a soft haze above the sea, the rich air smelling of salt and fish. There is power in the muscular strength of the sea. Yet, at times, there is nothing softer, and this was a soft day.

Georgianna is a Chumash and Papago woman. As two Native citizens of this continent, we sat beside the great movement of sea and talked. As we sat, I remembered reading once that the Papago, living far from the sea, take a yearly journey to the ocean for salt. They call ocean a power of high order, a mysterious being, and so we sat beside that element considered to be healing, and we talked, knowing its currents, like ours, are created by elements powerfully beyond us, the spin of earth, the pull of moon, the storms far away.

▲   ▲   ▲

THAT DAY WE were at the thresholds of water, of language, and even of our own bodies. We talked about the healing we have each sought. Georgianna and I inhabited a similar territory, the world of physical pain, my own from a neuromuscular disease. Perhaps the ocean and our words could offer us hope. As humans have always done, we searched for meaning in illness, for an understanding. In the past, our infirmities might have been a taboo broken, a god offended, an intrusion of evil spirits, souls lost and stolen, gods punishing us for our actions, or the crossing of a path once struck by lightning. Even now it is a world populated with the invisible: microbes, bacteria, and viruses. We haven't changed all that much in the very great passage of time. With all our medical discoveries, we are still, like the clay woman, coming apart and breaking.

Humans have always been victims of disease, awaiting the dread unknown of death. And we have placed everything possible in its path, incantations, prayers, and pleadings. People have consumed heavy metals, used barbers or leeches to bleed them. They have even written on paper and swallowed it, hoping words taken into the body might be an antidote.

No longer do most people use amulets, bromides, and the sulfurs of the past to heal them. Now we look toward injections, pills, surgery, adjustments, even changes in thinking. In this country, we have even tried to make the elderly disappear from our sight. We've hoped, by song or belief, to save ourselves from what can happen to a human body, even from witnessing it.

As humans we've thought, like Georgianna and me, that if we find a story, tell it well, it will contain a thread out of the dark human labyrinth into light and wholeness. And if we can trace its origins, we think there is a way to reach healing. But when the world itself is sick, there are no stories and there is no place to retreat. This is a world with a new order of disease. Even the ocean, considered life-giving, is no longer healthy.

Soon Georgianna and I fell quietly into the rhythm of the shining ocean. It is not insignificant that we are Native women, because history lives cell-deep within us. And as we talked we added history to the list of causes of illness. The split of cultures has come to dwell in our skin.

It was the past that began our friendship in the first place, that day we first met and visited. In the museum shop, where the clay woman was displayed, we discovered of each other that we both were born "back in the olden days." We remembered an older way of life, one before cars, days with horses and wagons. The way my Chickasaw grandparents lived in Oklahoma when I was a child was the same way Georgianna's family lived about that same time. The fifties and sixties for indigenous people were like the early 1900s for the new Americans. I think of this now, this connection to another time and what it has meant to our lives to feel ourselves so newly come to the modern world, and how comforting it has been for me to have someone other than my sister and cousins to share this with. We have been so shaped by our lives in a different, earlier America, as if we are not fully of this time.

Looking back so many decades later, I think of that life as rich. For me, as a young person in Oklahoma with my grandparents, the nights with fireflies, the sound of the horses greeting each other, their heavy feet on earth, was the best of life. Our grandma, who'd never cut her hair in all her life, cooked Chickasaw pashofa, a food something like hominy, in a large black kettle on the woodstove. Some hot nights we made ice cream in a hand-crank machine using salt, cream, vanilla, and ice we bought from the icehouse in Ardmore, Oklahoma. Afterwards we children all chased each other with ice, to put it down the shirts and blouses of our cousins.

This world was my foundation. I know it more solidly as I age. It became my life, my identity as a woman. I was a solitary, unhappy child in other places and ways, but not in Oklahoma, where my grandfather paid us to be quiet. "Dimes," I once said, and another woman said, "Your granddaddy was rich. We only got nickels." All I know is that my life has never fully existed in the other, mainstream, America. There is a larger sphere of our context to be taken into consideration. It is in the America that reveres the land, that is attached, like the clay woman, to where we dwell. Georgianna and I are from the America of other, first, people. Like the broken woman who watches over the injured world, we are connected to the land.

▲　　　▲　　　▲

AND SO, SITTING together on the edge of water and sand, we told each other our stories, Georgianna and I. Not only were words bridges of affinity between us, but in our offering of words it seemed something was born. A spoken story is larger than one unheard, unsaid. In nearly all creation accounts, words or songs are how the world was created, the animals sung into existence. Why should it be different for human lives? We are, as Kiowa writer N. Scott Momaday said, made of words.

▲   ▲   ▲

IN MY LIFE I've listened, sometimes without deep enough attention, to people talk about illness, their aches, pains, and failing bodies. From the age of fifteen, I worked full-time. My first jobs were in nursing homes. In my mind's eye, I can still see many of the patients. There was Stella, a white woman with long, braided hair. Her room was at the end of a dark hall by an exit sign. I remember her as lively. She exercised every day. There was another woman who spoke only about her long-gone man, Banks. There was Billie the cowboy who always wanted me to put the children to bed and come back. In a room by the front entry was a woman who called me Mary, and out of sympathy I pretended to be this Mary; it made her happy. Next to her was a white-haired woman who had been a judge, and next to her was an Apache woman who had been in a car accident and wore a full body cast. There was a woman whose son had drowned. She died of liver damage caused by years of drinking her grief. And then there was another woman whose face and body I still see. Her white hair had bangs. She was in great pain, but she was a Christian Scientist and didn't believe in medication. She would cry "Dear God," over and over, until finally she consented to taking pain medication, and then she'd feel she had failed.

While I, like other many others, wanted to alleviate the suffering of other people, I was young and vital, thriving. I had not enough understanding of the ill. I cared for them, but from the distance of youth, my own body was shielded from pain. Nor did I understand memory.

The aged remember the past most strongly. It is why the woman called me Mary. Short-term memory gives way to long-term and it is the far past that is most present. Things pass before people's minds as they age, old memories overlie the new. My father relates this story: He was a young orderly, new to the army, taking care of a general who had broken a strike of miners and sent them away in railroad cars. He saw, over and over, the hand of a girl caught in the door. He called out, in his last days, "Open the door," and then a door opened and he saw, at his own ending, his sin, that of closing strikers into a railroad car. Then the door closed.

Watching Over the Sea

RACHEL CARSON WAS a woman who watched over the world. She called the shore, where Georgianna and I sat, a place of compromises, conflicts, and eternal change. The shore is a place of endings and beginnings, of constant movement and change. In the ocean's fathomless depths is the roughness that takes mountains down into grains of sand, the dead into nothing, or almost so. The ocean swallows a beach one year and returns it another.

And so we sat, Georgianna and I. On the skin of water, infant fish float in the clear sheltering sacs of their eggs, an eye visible, a curved fin, spine, the beating hearts we humans share, afloat, moving into these bodies like shells taken up by hermit crabs, the very precious being of all our bodies.

We watched sea wracks, the tips of them, and other alive plants in the water reach above the surface now and then. There are colonies of plants, underworld forests bending with currents and tides, animals grown from single cells. Milk-blue squid have descended, waiting for night when they will rise to the surface. All this, in two parts hydrogen, one part oxygen, such simple components, but unable to be duplicated in any lab.

In all this, our human illnesses seemed a small event. But to us it was large, a determining, shaping factor in our lives.

▲   ▲   ▲

WE WALKED BAREFOOT at water's edge, the sand warm and soft. The rockweeds had washed up, succulent thick strands and bulbs of copper light, alive on white sand. Their weight shelters forms of life hidden beneath them, waiting for the next tide to take them back. At this marginal world there is a kind of peace between different and opposing elements. I want to learn it.

The Loon

AS WE WALKED barefoot beyond the place of smoothed lava stones, we spotted the loon, still and quiet, a sitting island nestled in a sea of sand. As we neared it, its stillness was a hold in time that said something was wrong. The red-eyed loon sat, breath raising and lowering its body, as if resigned to death. Having been around illness and death, I recognized the sinking appearance of its body, as if it were subject to more gravity than the healthy, the weight and skin drawn toward earth. The loon did not protest when I slipped my hand beneath it and felt the sludge, and the smell of oil, thick and black, stuck to his feathers. The bird was between places, stopped in its migration, and also between life and death.

How did the loon know this migration, this flight that brought him here through light, the magnetic pull of earth, and ancestral knowings? The loon's government of ancient ways, from its body alone, said, "Take to air, to another sea. Leave tundra and winter." It flew to places of earth between cold and warmth. Even then as it sat, its blood, its bones, were telling it to go, and yet it could not.

The bird did not struggle when I lifted it. The bird was overly light even though its weight had settled. In patches around the loon, the beach, too, was black with what had washed in from the spills. Its fate was interwoven with our own human fates in this world we humans have diminished because we have failed to understand how each thing connects with all the rest.

▲   ▲   ▲

WE CARRIED THE loon to a trailer set up at the beach, but the young man who worked there was getting off work. There was nothing he could do, he said, as he locked the door and left. Maybe he was young, maybe heartless, or perhaps he'd already seen such devastation that he no longer noticed or cared about a single bird. In any case, our choices were few. We could leave the loon, or we could search for a veterinarian who knew about wild birds and oil spills.

So we set out in search of help. In a box, we carried the bird to the home of Georgianna's sister, who lived nearby. From there, we called a wildlife officer. After many calls, we finally located a rehabilitator who knew what to do. I left a message. Then there was the long waiting for her to return our call. While we waited, I worried about the fumes being toxic for the bird. Also, I was incompetent here, a land person, having never been close to oil slicks and ocean.

I admired the loon, his wings, the amazing boundaries and

adaptations of form that contain the life, the blueprint of his bones that knew to be hollow, to shape themselves in their way, the magnficent body grown from an egg, the feet that cannot walk on land, the fine, meticulous formation of black and white feathers.

The loon's beauty and power, most think, is in its voice. When I lived in the north, I heard the cries of the loon rising easily and quickly up an octave, down again. Like the voice of the wolf. Their cries made me think that they listened to each other.

▲   ▲   ▲

AS WE WAITED for the call, Georgianna's sister returned home from a surgery and lay on the couch. We visited with her while waiting for the phone call, leaving the bird in a box on the kitchen table. Soon their mother came inside and joined us. She is a beautiful Papago woman. She sat in her chair at the end of the table, wearing a white blouse, gathered at the neck, her black-and-gray hair back from her face and soft.

▲   ▲   ▲

GEORGIANNA'S FATHER IS Chumash. I met him and her mother on that earlier trip to California where I bought the clay woman. He was quite elderly now. The back door opened and he came in, a man grown small with age, gentleness a part of his face, hands, body. A man from the old villages along the sea, the ones that had been dislocated by gold-seekers and priests and then by overlarge cities and developments. He was an indigenous artist, a traditional shell-worker and a carver whose works are in museums. "I fell down," he said, and he went on to say that he had slipped outside and that his back, which had been painful, was much the better for the fall. "It's a funny thing," he said, touching his shoulder. Georgianna's mother began to cry. Tears were the work of the heart at this moment. The pain and sorrow were not only about the man falling to the ground of space and time and history, not only about her daughter on the couch. It was not only the loon, but that the bird and its history held resonances of all these other things. It touched on other worlds and even the historical past, the way we, as Indian people, were not intended to survive.

▲   ▲   ▲

FOR MYSELF, BEING one of those people who survived, my tribal identity has always been chasing after me, to keep its claims on my body and heart. I can't escape and be whole and real. As if I am the lung and it is the air breathing me in and out like waves of the ocean, rhythms and cycles of wind. It is the blood; I'm just the container. It is the ocean. It carries me and I float. It is something Native people can never explain to those who don't know it, and I have given up trying to do so. As with life, as with water, attempts to explain it slip through fingers and minds. I only know that the heart and the mind are created by culture, past and present. And probably so is the spirit, though I'd like to think it was not so, because I'd like to think that there is a consciousness of the value of life inherent in all people. I've concluded over the years that the two ways, Native and European, are almost impossible to intertwine, that they are parallel worlds taking place at the same time, bridges only sometimes made, allowing for a meeting place of lives.

This is all I can say. There is something that we Indian people share at the deepest levels of ourselves, and it is a living, present thing. It is there in the dreaming, in a voice always at the ear, an old song, the land we come from, but also in the clay and breakings of earth, woman, bird.

That day, waiting for the call from the woman who could help the loon, I thought of all of us in the room, not only the textures of our infirmities, but of what had been stolen from us and broken. There was an intelligence. There were other ways of knowing which included rituals and ceremonies. We had great knowledge of plants, minerals, and medicines. American Indians who'd survived tens of thousands of years witnessed the great destruction of our knowledge systems, which included knowledge of ecosystems. All of us in that room knew that western medicine, even with its best powers, could not heal us, perhaps not even the delicate loon, whose song was beautiful and haunting.

But how much we want healing, the true wholeness of being in our place, in the world. Every one of us knew it, and we knew, too, that we were powerless, the loon and all of us waiting for the ring of the phone without which we would be even more lost. And I think, What kind of people would we have been if we had walked on? What then would be our own creaturehood? What then could we have called ourselves?

▲   ▲   ▲

THE HOUSEHOLD SOON filled up with grandchildren and great-grandchildren. I moved the loon to a back bedroom, because working with wildlife, I've seen birds die merely from stress. The loon was silent and still, there in the house of what might have, at other times, been his enemies.

The young people were wearing trucker's hats and tennis shoes, carrying food, and carrying a beloved new baby who soon found herself in the loving arms of her grandmother. I admired the baby, a being of the future. The baby had two extra fingers on each hand, so beautiful and perfect and useful, but fingers that would mark her as different, and because of that, however perfect they were, they might be removed to keep her from the trauma of difference. And I thought of the Navajo uranium miners, how they grew extra fingers, sometimes from an arm or elbow. Their bodies changed and mutated in one short lifetime, their own. Their pictures were carried about this country by their widows, who traveled a decade or more ago, hoping for, asking for, justice, which was never forthcoming. Even when they won their lawsuit they were never paid.

▲   ▲   ▲

FINALLY, THE PHONE rang. It was the call we'd been waiting for. It put us in action. Georgianna, the bird, and I drove to a suburb where the woman who took care of the loons lived. She said we should have placed the bird in cloth. So easy and clear, I was embarrassed not to have thought of it.

▲   ▲   ▲

I THINK OF that day now. It was a day of meetings, the coming together of water and land, the bridged distances of private worlds and histories. Bird. Friends. Tribes. Something had been righted by this accidental pilgrimage and these incomplete journeys.

Our healing, we both knew, was connected to this other healing, as woman to land, as bird to water. We are together in this, all of us, and it's our job to love each other, human, animal, and land, the way ocean loves shore, and shore loves and needs the ocean, even if they are different elements.

Georgianna's father called me, in Chumash, the Girl Who Saved the Loon. I tell this not to make myself look good, but to reveal our values. This is what we love about our elders, that they honor us when we care, not when we win, but when we look after the earth and show compassion. In truth, I can say that I was also as broken as the Bruja Who Watched Over the World, as damaged as the loon.

The loon lived, but not long after this, Georgianna's father died. He was greatly missed by his loving family. His words at his passage were "Oh what a beautiful light to do shell work by."

WATER: A LOVE STORY

Sea Level

IT MUST HAVE been a desert person who said from dust we come to dust we return, because, for most of us, water is the true element of our origin. Broken birthwaters signal our emergence into the air world, and through our lifetimes it is water that sustains us, water that is the human substance, the matter of cells.

Some years ago I turned my attention to water. Perhaps, as people have done since the beginning of time, I went to water to seek a cure, and became enamored of the deep. I was drawn to it in all its forms, ocean, river, lake, swamp. In the dry country where I live, water comes to us as rain and snow and trickling creek, so I paid frequent visits to this mother element in her other shapes. I swam in the ocean, overcoming—but only cautiously—my fear of the depths my human feet could not touch. I sat in mangrove swamps watching as the trees changed salt water into fresh. I waded around the "eye of water," the entrance where spring water rises from beneath the surface world, and floated underground rivers inside white limestone caverns. I paddled kayaks in the unsought but welcome presence of dolphins and whales, including a female humpback who gave birth where my friend and I sat. I submerged myself in hot springs and visited glaciers, and looked into the tragically endangered world of the paling, breathing coral reefs. I looked into a kelp bed, down into the dark, cold water, at thumbnail-size jellyfish, white and pulsing. With my sister I walked from the edge of sea to the black caves that, at low tide, are full and open with life as the tide goes out in its endless back and forth. There, in tide pools at the edge of the sea, were worlds of beauty, starfish, orange and alive, anemones, seaweed, and patient waiting, a sort of creature faith that water would return.

I myself am a failure at faith. And also impatient at waiting. But I do know this, that thoughts and visions of water are always the same. They are about beneath and inside, like the watershed which travels underground and the water that falls into it. And so, despite all my outward journeys, mostly I frequented water in an inner way, looking at the depths of my own life, my body of brine moisture and blood rivers. But there, too, in keeping with the nature of water, I realized that my feet would not ever touch bottom.

The inside of a person is more mysterious than the inside of the world. It's just that we seem to inhabit it more plainly. Still, who knows it? Our human theories do not stretch large enough to pass easily through the inner territory. We are too fluid to pin down, and passing through our lives like water, we cannot easily be called back as we fall into self, time, and what seems like destiny. Like water that, in its oceanic destiny, follows a fierce journey of its own desires through rivers, sea waves, and even beneath ground, we each have our own journey, too.

It is only now, from within my own body, and from the other half of a century, that I can begin to see myself. I am just now becoming a human being, as many tribes say. And I am becoming a person old and joyous and vulnerable in new ways. Half a century is a great beginning, and still the mystery of the self is there. Like water, I rush toward a destiny, a balance, a harmony. I call it sea level.

Water is the medium through which things travel. It wishes to return to sea level, a still point. It slips through human hands. It falls from the sky. This is true not only in the great seas people cross over, but also in our human deaths when the body gives in to fluids and yeasts. At the end, the body breaks down to water. I've seen it, the swelling of a human with fluid, the running, the pneuma, the body with life sliding away from it, becoming once again the ocean, the water. Not dust, as claimed by that desert person.

▲   ▲   ▲

I SUPPOSE I have always been caught in the waves and tides of time, place, and history. There were my grandmothers and grandfathers, whose pairings, some loving and some miserable, brought me to life. Then there is the body with its innumerable waves of memory, its own destiny, its own tides and ways a single person is shaped.

Perhaps another reason I looked toward water and the sea was my own history, a remembered event of my own passage and crossing from Europe to America when I was fifteen.

The passage of which I speak took place in 1963. It was the first ship of my life, the first sight of an ocean, my first experience on any kind of water except a puddle or creek, or the tanque of my Chickasaw grandparents, their waterhole, where I played and imagined the past history of our tribe, the Indian people who are yet my defining world.

I was fifteen and it was a nine-day journey across the sea in dark January. The Atlantic Ocean carried me from Bremerhaven, Germany, to New York, an island of rock that had been exchanged for beads, mirrors, the rare baubles and bangles valuable to those who had no concept of what land and paper meant.

We were returning from Germany, where I'd lived with my family. My father had been in the army. He was an enlisted man, a sergeant, but now we were leaving Germany a few months early because he had a medical discharge for heart disease.

The journey was a suspended moment in life for me, a tear in the fabric of time. I was unformed matter, pre-woman. As a girl I was like clay still unfired by time and life and thought, unconscious even of myself. Even before we set out to cross an ocean, I had already been living in a world of betweens. Not just between cultures, as a mixed-blood girl, and times, but in other ways, too. I'd existed in a middle world between girlhood and womanhood. It wasn't limbo. It was a life more empty than that. Now I traveled between places, between continents, between lives. This region would become the region I would always seek out, even as an adult, in my work, my interests, my loves. Perhaps "between" was, is, at the root of my very existence.

▲   ▲   ▲

I WAS FIFTEEN and my first love was now over. I was grieving the loss deeply but I was also grateful and relieved that there was such distance between myself and the place where that love unfolded. It left me fresh and hopeful, feeling I could become someone who wasn't shunned, that crossing this dark water I might have a chance to start my young life over. I was leaving something behind, not just going toward another history. I was myself so small and young. As an Indian girl, I was moving toward my own continent, my place, bound to the American continent and all that transpired before my birth. This time my own story was added to it.

He, Robert, touched me in so many ways. My famished skin. He took me to stores and bought me the necessities, a warm coat that was nearly black and had soft white hairs in it, warm boots. He said I would be pretty by the time I was twenty, as if I had something to look forward to in the far adulthood I might one day reach. For then I was plain, wore no makeup, and was still too young to give a thought to clothes or figures or appearances. He gave chocolates to me and to my mother, who thought him so handsome she could understand why I was in love with him even though I was only twelve years old.

At the time, it was love and I needed it. I would have fought for it, and I did. He was a human who longed for me. Standing under the clothesline one day, behind the military quarters, singing a love song, he wrote on my hand, "I love you." He was the first person to say these words to me. It was spelled out inside my palm, as if he were too afraid to say the words. I read the touch. His finger on my palm was, as it turned out, a gesture that told some of my future.

▲   ▲   ▲

OUR RELATIONSHIP, ROBERT'S and mine, had been a marriage. No one had ever said, "I pronounce you." It just evolved this way. The relationship became an illegal, common-law connection of a man and a twelve-year-old girl.

The agreement was unspoken and didn't exist on paper. But it was understood and it was everything marriage means. Nothing was said about it, by any of us, my parents or myself. I wore a ring. I loved a grown man twice my age.

Now, on the ship, traveling toward myself and my own continent, I felt my life opening. But the truth was, like all travelers, I brought my history with me. The affair of love that I wanted to escape lived in me as things live in water, beneath the surface, hidden and ever-changing with currents, tides, and shifting directions. Nor was I fixed on what lay ahead. I couldn't navigate or follow stars. I knew nothing of currents, tides, or nautical miles. I was innocent of the sea and the movement beneath us and even of my own inner world and the directions I might someday travel. I was trusting without a reason to be. I only knew my heart was wounded, hopeful, and sad, all at the same time. On this large ocean, the ocean that became the route to the unknown, I was only carried, simply carried, across the Atlantic like driftwood tossed about by another will, or ice on a surface choppy with change. Nor would I understand, even over many decades, the life I had left. I was between, only between, the shores of two continents, and I was held up by that element "water."

But I felt that I moved toward something. I was in a sea of becoming. I had a beginner's sense of the depths of this sea, but it had not yet come to words. As a child I was at a loss for words anyway. Silence had been my way of being. I had a fear of speaking, and it had been a problem in school. I was too shy to say "Here" at roll call or even to raise a hand when my name was called. In school, I was too young for my age. Away from school I was already a woman in many other ways, cooking, ironing, not only with a woman's jobs and duties at that time, but also in my union with a man. And now it was as if my small life was in some way being tossed about at sea. Maybe it was the place where words emerge from silences. All I know is that water is what you cannot carry without a container. And the life of mine, still so young and uncontained, was already shaped and being shaped beyond what I could know. I was fifteen and in a tipping vessel. It was winter and gray and stormy. Enormous white-crested waves sent shoes sliding across the floor. Drinking glasses spilled. People fell against walls. I liked my little upper bunk, from which I could look down and watch my father shave as he stood at the cabin sink in front of a mirror made of distorted, polished metal, looking at his imperfect reflection.

Soon, everyone but me was sick. My mother, father, and brother were unable to get up from their bunks. But I had sea legs the others seemed to lack, and the rising and falling of the boat was something of a comfort to me. I thrived on its movement. And so, while they remained isolated and sick in the dark cabin of the sea vessel, I was given freedom.

I carried oranges and saltines to my seasick family, but once I served them, I was without parents and sisterly duties. In the dark gray coat Robert had bought me, I stood on the deck and watched the water and sky. I watched the occasional spumes of whales in the distance, and felt the cold spray on my face, my hair thick with dampness, when I stood outside for hours watching the lead-gray water. Inside, I roamed the fresh-painted corridors of the ship. Even with beige walls, it seemed dark inside as we rocked back and forth. I watched people, made a friend, smoked her cigarettes. Together we looked at the dark men who worked on the boat and to whom I was attracted.

In the middle of the sea, and for the first time in my memory, I felt inside myself a cellular aliveness. It was a freedom. I felt whole, alone, unafraid, and nearly a woman. I reached a kind of balance on that journey, a bodily joy. Even rocked by the ocean, it was as if I'd been water all along and had finally reached sea level and could rest in myself, floating there in the middle of sea.

Atlantic

THE OCEAN WE traveled, you might say, belonged mythically to the child daughter of the man, Atlas, who held up the sky. She, Atlantis, was the one who, alone of all the gods or people of mythic flesh, knew the depths of ocean.

Atlas, the father, was forced to carry the weight of heaven and its unholy history, its deadly consequences on those who did not aspire toward it. In most mythic stories, the sky has been associated with the male, with imagined places, and with the early gods. It seems fitting, destined even, that the daughter of Atlas would have to go where her father did not, could not, travel. She went downward beneath the rocking of tides, descending in the waters of darkness, to the pulsing life of the sea, the beautiful floor made of minuscule diatoms and fallen lives.

▲   ▲   ▲

IN THE NORTHERN tribes, Sedna, the Sea Mother, "the one down there," is one of the denizens of the deep. By many names, she has ruled over the dark, inner world of sea depths and water animals in the northernmost terrains. She is a sea-spirit woman of pure being, one who fell to the bottom.

There are different versions of Sedna's life and fate. She descends into the ocean and in the descent is changed. She learns becoming. In one story, her father married her to an old homely man who lived on an island. As her father left, she tried to go home with him, begging and holding on to her father's boat. Unable to loosen her grip, he cut off her fingers. Out of her lost fingers, the sea animals grew, whales, seals, walruses, and narwhals. Through her wounding, something else, other lives, was born.

Indwelling

WATER IS A door and you pass through and are beneath. That is the human relationship with it since the beginning of time. I loved the movement of the waves on that passage as I traveled toward an unknown future and away from a past, the flying fish leaping in unison, silver and strangely commanded from inside themselves. And from the deck of the ship, in the evenings, from a protected place, I watched the sun descend as if to light the underwater realm. Whatever was beneath us, the deep and fathomless mystery of it, it seemed I knew in some way, as if I knew there were giant fish and squid, things most of us never guess. It would be what saved me, those depths I spent the rest of my life seeking. I searched in a way so many others never try, as if a foot touching down against the bottom could finally push me to the surface. But it would be decades before I knew I had survived.

Now, thirty-five years later, I can still feel the quality of air on that voyage, still smell the life-filled scent of the sea, and recall how small and storm-tossed we were, and how much I loved it. Now, when I look at water, I know a bit of what resides there. I have seen inside both the water of the world and the waters of the human spirit.

▲   ▲   ▲

DURING THAT CROSSING I would change. It was more than a rite of passage, more than a journey over fertile water in which there were uncountable eggs with eyes and spines and tails in them, schools of silver fish and jellies all unseen by me. This journey was the first reckoning, the first knowledge I felt of a woman's body and spirit. It was a time of reflection, of light returned to the eye. It was a place, like the sea, that had no bottom, so anything was possible. In this beautiful solitude and silence was the quickening of the soul of an unhappy girl.

▲   ▲   ▲

BEFORE WE BOARDED the ship, my relationship with Robert was already over, though not officially. I knew it, felt it, already, from inside, even though it would be months before I received the final letter from him after his return to Little Rock. On the night he left Germany, before we did, I knew it was the last time I would see him. I felt it in my body as he departed, as I watched him, the soldier I loved, step into a dark train in Germany and head off on the first leg of his trip back to the United States. I cried without consolation as the Germans in the train station watched with keen interest my American display of grief and racking sobs, the awkwardness and naked expression we possess. I knew I would never see his face again in all my life. The grief I felt was enormous. That night in Germany as the train carried Robert away, as we drove back home to the military base in the rain, I opened the window and looked upward, my face turned toward the dark heavens, and I let the cold rainwater fall on my skin. I sat looking up, eyes closed, as we waited in the car near the river for the bridge that raised itself up for ships too large to pass beneath. And then the bridge lowered.

▲　　　▲　　　▲

I WAS TWELVE at the time of this relationship I call marriage. Mercifully he was a tender, gentle lover, a kind man. Still, my body was too young for it. I'd always been susceptible to colds, tonsilitis, and infections, but added to this now was blood in my urine, and fainting spells that, I suppose, were the result of emotional trauma.

While most of the other twelve-year olds were playing, I fell into life as something of an adult, doing housework, taking care of other people's children, and myself trying to become pregnant, to make a family. The consequences were many. I was shunned by schoolmates and neighbors for my life with the soldier. I was an outcast. There were jokes and name-calling. The school made calls home; there was a sense that something was terribly wrong. At the time I sought refuge in religion. I believed a small and childish version of the Bible and God. Religion, as a girl, became my world. It was all I had and I needed it in order to survive. I used it to save myself. God understood me.

And Robert, who was the son of a prostitute, brought life to our family. He represented, in an odd way, something like salvation and energy. In the evenings, in a previously quiet family, we now worked puzzles together, or we played cards, or a

German game, "Mensch Argeres Dich Nicht," or we played Monopoly, which, to my happiness, I always won. On Sundays, all together, with my parents and little brother, we went to play bingo at the NCO club. In a previously quiet world, he was my life, all of it, in every way. He, with his seemingly swaggering walk, was the focus of my world.

▲   ▲   ▲

MY GOAL IN our lovemaking, as I said, was to have a baby. I needed something or someone else to love, an escape into my own home with him and marriage. I had no other dreams of a future, I was a child who had been suicidal for as far back as I could remember, praying each night for death, as if I'd inherited all the wounds of an American history along with a family which hadn't yet learned to love, touch, or care. As an impoverished child with my experience and history, a baby was the most I could hope for.

Looking back, even now, the two sides of this relationship baffle me; it was love and it was also wrong.

▲   ▲   ▲

AS GIRLS, WE are so easy to love. So forbidden and tender and sweet-smelling. So simple and easy. There are no arguments. There is no self. A few of the other girls I went to school with were also in unusual relationships, and I made friendships only with those who, like myself, were injured in some way and had sought relationships in ways others thought inappropriate. There was Paula, who, whether for self-protection or self-consciousness, never removed her coat, even in the classroom, and whose mother seemed like a witch. Mary, who was engaged to a thirty-five-year-old soldier, and Celia, who said she had sex with her father, brother, and a parade of young soldiers who frequented their house. She was a twelve-year-old woman so much older than I. She was designed to look sexual. Thin eyebrows. Makeup. Revealing clothing and movement. Sex, I believe now, was probably the only power she wielded in her wretched, abused life.

I wasn't a sexualized child. I was unself-conscious about my body. Unlike Celia and many of the girls of today, I hadn't thought about what might be provocative. Nor was I familiar with the kinds of men and boys stationed in Germany. I hadn't heard most swear words. But suddenly I was surrounded by men hanging out windows. They were staring at me in lunchrooms. Men who would play at war during the Cuba missile crisis, while we dependents were ordered to pack all our primary goods, socks, food, coats, list what we were leaving behind, and prepare to drive to safety in Switzerland. I was surrounded by boys and men who would soon go to Vietnam, some of whom, on a training mission in Germany, raped and killed the chickens of a German farmer. This always terrorizes me, that there was something about military men when they were together that made them dangerous.

▲   ▲   ▲

I WAS, AS a child, painfully shy and vulnerable, and unable to speak. I wanted to be invisible and I had not developed well. I was a depressed, neglected child. My teeth had rotted, black and decayed, and other students teased me, taunting me with the unkind names children put together. I see that my life was shaped by a poverty of the heart, the lack of present love, which left me open to love from other places, because I was a child untouched by mother's hands, a child so disturbed as to have had almost no language. I say this now, looking back, knowing full well that my mother cooked for us and did all that was considered her duty, yet could not love.

Now, years later, I realize that it is easier to survive financial hardship than to survive emotional poverty. So when the relationship with Robert began, it had been bounty for such a hungry child.

But at fifteen, traveling that godly ocean, the ship was a sanctuary. I was contained, bound up and surrounded by life and water. I felt safer in the middle of a storm in a floating vessel at sea than I had ever been before that voyage, than I would feel for many years after it. Everything was tied down, so even if the boat tossed, there was an assurance of safety, and it seemed that in a tipping boat I somehow had my bearings. The walls of the ship, the keel and bow, were not as ovewhelming as life on land. Even the men whose looks I admired were too fine to flirt with a girl my age, and that, too, was a relief, although as I look backward now from so many years later, I know I would have offered myself to them, thinking it was love.

▲   ▲   ▲

I HAD TRAVELED to Germany a few years earlier by plane with my mother and brother. With softness toward my mother, I remember the details: En route her new gray dress had torn at the seams. My brother and I followed her through the Chicago airport as she looked for a needle and thread to mend it, then sat in the bathroom while she removed it and, in her slip, sewed. For her, the journey was stressful. Looking back, I feel such sympathy for her, kindness toward her, the way she wanted to be beautiful for my father, the way when we arrived, my brother was sick with the stomach flu. We moved into a place that had no heat but a coal stove, no refrigerator, and much fear for a woman like my mother, for she was vulnerable in a place of another language and people she believed stared at her, the foreigner.

▲　　　▲　　　▲

WITH ROBERT, I did not do what others did. I wasn't like them. I had no edges, borders, walls, no sense of what was wrong or right in love. There was not enough mind inside me yet. As a child I was permeable and I'd been starved for a soft human hand, love, and it was a hunger now fulfilled by Robert, so I wanted this relationship as the hungry want food. I would not have given it up. There was nothing that would have been able to keep me away from him, and perhaps my parents knew this, so they did not end the relationship, and perhaps, too, there was an element of fate.

▲　　　▲　　　▲

IN THE WATERS of memory, something old and bewildered floats upward and comes into full view, and it is seen as clear. Thirty-five years later I returned to this place in Germany by air, train, and rented car. I went back to the little once-army town that was now abandoned military buildings. Now it was empty, but in my memory it was full. It had the usual appearance of a "base," the long bowling alley, the cheap construction, the stucco quarters we had lived inside, drab cement wall on one side. On the other was the motor and ambulance pool where my father had worked, and where I could see him from our kitchen window.

▲   ▲   ▲

RETURNING, I FOUND the place by feel, my arms turning the car all these years later. As if by magic. I don't know how the body remembers and contains the past, but it does. I'd forgotten that the town, Wertheim, was a place of beauty, of a river passage, a castle, a hill that contained flowers and food crops and red poppies. I found first the little town of Urphar at the peaceful river where I used to sit and watch the houseboats pass, laundry hanging on their clotheslines. The place my father had caught a large pike and eels. The family ran a tile works and still do. They had been so grateful for the fish my father gave them, I recall, that they returned the favor by giving us a tub of pastries and wines. And now, visiting, all of us were old. The young woman so looked like her mother, I almost thought nothing had changed. They remembered me by the pike. I tried to converse with them in my poor German. The house was clean, improved, with new flowers at the window boxes, a hiking trail at the river. How beautiful was the town I had forgotten, with its flesh-colored stones and plaster, the cobblestone streets and green hills.

▲   ▲   ▲

THE ARMY BASE now contained some immigrants from another world, dislocated people seeking refuge from wars and other catastrophes. People sitting on the outskirts of any place, seemingly aimless, seemingly without work, trying to survive wars, military incursions, famines of bodies and souls. As I drove through the entryway to the base, the little hut where always before a military policeman would check our license plates and identifications, one man blew a kiss toward me and my friend as if to remind me of the sexual desire of the men who had once resided there, calling and whistling at the young girls when we were yet children.

As I looked about me, it seemed as if the place itself was haunted by the past, as if memory resided in the ground itself and I became only an interpreter of it. I stood on the ground below the "quarters" where we had lived and looked up into the tan government building, into the broken window from which I'd once looked out. Now there was darkness behind that window, emptiness in the place where I'd once danced in the sunlight that came through the window. Then, it had been furnished more beautifully than any place we'd ever had before or after. It was the place where as a child, I lifted my skirt for the young man who had paid for that skirt, and I remember it so clearly, the cloth emerald-green cotton with black-and-gold designs in it, a small pattern like a mosaic. It was a gathered skirt whose color I thought beautiful when I was a girl, and I also wore high heels too tall to walk in, so that I looked tilted-forward and silly.

▲   ▲   ▲

THE BUILDING DESIGN is still in my mind, as are the smells that once filled the stairwells of this building where we lived, the voices that were, like us, racially mixed, an Eskimo woman married to a white man, Italians whose cooking filled the air with garlic and sauces, a pair of Hispanic sisters who, as was common in those days, called themselves "Spanish," and who taught me to call and ask their Spanish-speaking mother, "*Está Myrna en la casa?*"

▲   ▲   ▲

NOW I WALKED the same streets I had walked as a girl, sur-
prised they were so narrow, so short in distance. The army post
was so small a place, so closed, as if closure might forgive it all
its sins and histories and forces, allied and broken. Its foreign
army of Americans had not been there to keep peace so much
as to keep inside the German mind a memory of recent war,
to remind them of their guilt, their capacity for evil, but the
Americans had it, too.

I walked from the broken window of our apartment to the
abandoned barracks that housed the artillery squadron where
Robert, when I tried to end our relationship because he'd been
drinking, tried to commit suicide by cutting his wrists and
neck. I stood before the building remembering how I ran
toward him, entered that building of men where he bled. I
"flew," one of his friends said, to where he lay waiting for the
ambulance to arrive, his blood streaming out of him. It was the
night of a Christmas program and I'd been watching my little
brother sing. After that, I felt as if I was a child responsible for
the life of an adult man. Perhaps that was why, at fifteen, as I
stood on the ship for those days surrounded by gray and rocked
by the mother sea, I felt relief and alive and unbound.

As with Sedna, whose lost fingers became something unexpected, seals and whales, life sometimes emerges from pain.
She became an indweller of the sea and the depths. Just as
with Atlanta, it was indwelling and knowledge of the depths
that was her salvation. Still, I descend and my feet will never
touch bottom. But what is below and inside is a life-giving
power. Hidden worlds are only a door we pass through, and
water is perhaps the best place to find ourselves.

▲　　　　▲　　　　▲

BUT EVEN SO, traveling over an ocean, the immensity of it, I had no hint of what lay ahead for me. In pieces I arrived in America, a girl, I'd hoped, without a known history. But grief came with me, an anchor carried, dropped down now and then to hold me fast in depressions and sadness. There were tides and waves I wouldn't have guessed in my passage to America.

▲   ▲   ▲

PERSONAL HISTORY AND belief, I think, are not so far away from the histories of land, time and space, water, and exploitation. A child held up by water, I journeyed away from a broken human past. What I couldn't count on or know at that young age was what I carried with me, even though only a few pictures remain of Robert, in addition to those from my parents' movie camera. I was just one small girl in all history, on a wide ocean, on a ship toward an unkind America where once my ancestors had watched the cruel invaders disembark, where the arrivers had cut off the hands of the people and laughed as they tried, desperately unable, to help themselves. Some of the people did not survive. But, like the sea goddess, Sedna, those who did found that their hands and fingers grew something unexpected and not of their making. We Indian people who had inhabited the land of the fountain of youth had not been meant to survive and yet we did, some of us, carrying the souls of our ancestors, and now they speak through us. It was this that saved my life, that finally contained me. Or better said, I contained it.

▲   ▲   ▲

AS WITH SEDNA, the girl whose lost fingers became seals and whales, life sometimes comes out of tragedy. All human stories are this. In the north, in a world of ice, out of Sedna's pain, life was created. With Sedna, an inward dweller of the sea, as with the daughter of Atlas, it was indwelling that saved them; it was knowledge of the depths, and this is what stories try to teach us, even our own; that what's below and beneath and inside is a generative, life-giving power. I became an indweller. And hidden worlds are only a door we pass through beneath the difficult earth surface world.

I know there are forces and powers stronger than human and sometimes we chance to meet one, or one takes hold of us and moves us along. Water is one of these. Our ship on those nine days was a floating island with such inhabitants. I can yet smell the aftershave, the soap. I remember the night driving home, face to the rain. Now there are times I put water in a jar and look at it, clear, beautiful, and moon-loved element that it is. I think of it, an element that amazing, one that moves aside for us. Sometimes there is a wellspring or river of something beautiful and possible in the tenderest sense that comes to and from the most broken of children, and I was one of these, and whatever it was, I can't name, I can only thank. Perhaps it is the water of life that saves us, after all.

FALLING

For giving us the horse

we can almost forgive the alcohol

Almost

— CARROLL ARNETT

Gogisgi

The World in a Bottle

MY FATHER, WHO has a beautiful and content spirit, recently told me and a friend that I was one of the reasons he quit drinking. One night, when he was drunk and I was a baby, he was bouncing me on the bed and I fell on the floor, hitting my head. I cried for so long, he couldn't comfort me. He went to the icebox to get me some food and the only thing in it, he says, was Jim Beam. Some time after that he was in the hospital for a year with cirrhosis. A year is a very long time and my father, then, a far cry from the man who met my lovely mother, a handsome Indian man in a pinstripe suit who bowed to her so formally and asked her to dance. They won a jitterbug contest without even knowing it was a contest.

And there was his father, my grandfather; my aunt told me once about finding him passed out over a short, sharp fence near Ardmore, Oklahoma, the town where we went to buy ice for the icebox. My aunt, being kind, wanted to help him up, but my grandmother held her back. She told her that he might wake up fighting. And so they left him there. Some nights he slept on the streets in the town of Ardmore with the other lost and wounded men. Before this time, he had done well as a rancher and cowboy until legal problems, the Depression, foreclosures, and the closing of the banks took all his assets. This happened to most of the Chickasaws, who during the 1930s, if not earlier, found themselves landless.

The dust storms, sand, and harsh winds of a deforested, overworked Oklahoma covered and eroded lives. My grandfather became a man who had lost everything. He had even been betrayed by his own relatives; his brother once sold him a stolen car, and so, I think, he gave up and fell into poverty, where most of our tribe remained afterwards. He was not like the man in an early photograph, so vital, the man wearing a fine coat and hat, walking down the street. Instead, he was replaced by the one whose horse stood over him in the field when he fell to the ground, drunk. There is a great sadness in the loss of a man to a bottle. Yet it is not an uncommon story in Native America, where there were even greater losses than his, the loss of lives and an entire land, its languages, its theologies and their beauty.

Now, looking back, I wonder what either of them, my father, my grandfather, would have made of my own life in that same bottle-contained world if they could ever have known that I followed their pathway, the geography of drunkenness. I inherited, in my own way, their great loneliness and a portion of despair of our Indian America. I look at the few baby pictures of my first happy steps, the way I nearly ran as I learned not to fall. Later I would fall through a life, fall as my grandfather did upon the sharp fences and boundaries of an America whose dark ongoing history is still unbearable.

Falling: The Lost Years

ONE OF MY friends describes drinking as "the lost years." Many of us have had them. For some, like myself, the years have come to us from before our own life spans. I tell you this, as hard as it is; when I was young and drinking, there was a time I jumped out of a moving car. More than once I crawled through a field near the air base, my knees and thighs and legs scraped and torn by cactus needles and gravel. Or in a snowstorm without a coat, I would trip over railroad tracks. There was cheap red wine I drank in the mornings, and a boyfriend who coughed up blood, though we were very young.

I drank suicidally, peroxide, cough syrup, and I was not alone. A friend I worked with years later was one of the Indian girls recruited for elite Eastern girls' colleges in the late sixties. She was from Acoma, the oldest inhabited pueblo in what is now called New Mexico. She told me how she had wandered off from school one night into a white, snowing landscape of winter, had run naked and falling. Her spirit and body, if not her mind, understood the symbolism of the white world surrounding her, her vulnerability and difference within it.

▲   ▲   ▲

AS A YOUNG woman I was lost. I wanted to fall, to jump out of, or perhaps into, my own life. Whether through the door of a car, into a field, into the water of a lake or pool, or off a stool onto the floor of a bar, falling was the answer. My pain was inward and gravity its heaviness. Perhaps, without knowing it, I wanted and needed the earth and falling was the answer to a broken heart. In those long-ago days, I lay on the ground only because I was too drunk to get up. There I would lie on the life of the earth, on the heart of the mother with the rising plants and alive smell.

I see now, so many years later, that my heart was too tender to live in and survive this sharp-edged world. I was a drunk, not an alcoholic. For me, there was a difference; a drunk wants to lose the memory of every day. For her it is not a matter of being weak-willed, not even a territory of morality. It is—was—a way of not remembering. It was an escape from the pain of an American history.

Falling: Journey

THERE ARE ACCOUNTS of what our Indian world was like a little over a century ago. I've read the descriptions of Chickasaws before the Trail of Tears, the accounts of our beauty. Then, later, of our brokenness. Our people became so fragmented we are nearly tragically missing from the pages of history. But then, in those eyewitness accounts, it was said how beautiful we Chickasaws were. The men wore turbans and rode about on the famed, now mysteriously disappeared, almost mythic Chickasaw ponies who had to bend on a knee to eat the grasses because their necks were so short. There was much business at the time, supplies to be bought, items to be sold. The women, reportedly, were beautiful and serene and erect on their horses. Yet, as impressive in appearance as they were, they had no choice but to leave, being removed from Mississippi and Tennessee by legislation created by Andrew Jackson, and inside of them was hidden the grief at saying goodbye to our world. We touched the trees and leaves and said goodbye to the land and stones and wildlife. My ancestors had no notion of what they faced, how soon they would be hungry and pushed along by soldiers with bayonets, all of the beauty and capability gone. The Chickasaws left their own land, taking along even the pet cats and their litters of kittens; one woman was observed with a basket of puppies on her back, the mother dog following lightly behind. Such loving people. How soon there would be unbearable heaviness, soldiers tense, trying to keep the hungry men from hunting for deer to feed their people, elders, and children. I wonder how the Americans themselves ate on that trail called Betrayal, but it seemed they did. They were not the ones starved or despairing.

The federal government's plans in those days were to put all American Indian tribes in Oklahoma and build a wall around it, to keep us contained in the country which came to be called Indian Territory. It was then a place they didn't want.

The Chickasaws, with a reputation for never having been conquered, were seen later, by observers, along the Trail of Tears. The accounts were very different from those of our leaving. No longer did the men dash about. The horses were gone. The women wept. There were deadly epidemics. The watchers and writers of the time spoke of a changed people. Traveling alongside the Chickasaws were whiskey sellers, thieves, and horse-stealers intent on taking our well-bred, famous horses. We stopped, several times, unable to continue, frustrating the soldiers and American government. We were broken, almost forever, by grief and betrayal. We didn't even make it to what was to be our own land, but stopped in despair on Choctaw land, which was closer than our own. And for this breaking we had lost or been forced to sell our land, homes, horses, and world. We ended up owing the federal government $720,000 for the journey, charged for rations and assistance we hadn't even received, paying for the soldiers with their forceful use of bayonets.

At a Loss for Words

AS A YOUNG person coming from silences of both family and history, I had little of the language I needed to put a human life together. I was inarticulate to voice it, therefore to know it, even from within. I had an unnamed grief not only my own. I grew up with girls who cut or hit or burned themselves, as if it was a way to kill the self or to trade the pain of what resided within for external pain. There was never a language to say it, to form a geography or map or history of what had happened, not only in terms of history, but to ourselves. We grew in a silence. In those days there were no songs, no incantations, not even any prayers that would lay it out before us. We hurt ourselves; our own bodies became our language.

Words, I see now, are the defining shape of a human spirit. Without them, we fall. Without them, there is no accounting for the human place in the world. Language is an intimacy not only with others, but even with the self. It creates a person. Without it, in the dawn, in the dark of night, there is no way to know who or what we are.

One day the words came. I was an adult. I went to school after work. I read. I wrote. Words came, anchored to the earth, to matter, to the wholeness of nature. There was, in this, a fall, this time to a holy ground of a different order, a present magic, a light-bearing, soul-saving presence that illuminated my heart and mind and altered my destiny. Without it, who would guess what, as a human being, I might have become.

▲   ▲   ▲

WHAT IS A human being? I still ask myself each day. What is the self that, as a young woman, I had wanted to destroy it even though I would tenderly pick up an insect and move it, give it water, allow the wasps to live in my ceiling, and let in every stray or hurt animal? Why did I place more importance on their lives than on my own? But, in this reversed world, I did. I would cry as a child, looking up at the sky, asking God to take me back. I could see, even then, the full scope of the world that held so much suffering when it didn't have to.

▲   ▲   ▲

IT WAS ALWAYS unnamed, what I felt. I will never know exactly what saved me, except that I cried and asked whatever gods or beings or holiness that was in this world, asked the whole of creation, to take me, the hurt person, out of this body and let someone or something better inhabit it. I was young. As if I could make a bargain. I was not like those from other tribes, crying for a vision. But something did come in, and it saved me: a love for all nature, all life, a place created by words; I live in a place words built. I saw my humble, beautiful spirit, after a childhood where I wanted to die, I saw a soul worth living in spite of flaws and imperfections and history.

Falling, Touching Bottom, Pushing Off

THE LOWEST POINT, touching bottom enough to have a foot push me back to the surface, as if swimming, was what saved me.

There was a series of reasons for the end of my drunkenness over two decades ago. My marriage was ending. There were escalating fights and drinking. But the turning point was just a while after our divorce. I woke up after a party of folded napkins and everything just so. In the same week I had gone to a concert with a friend and looked down the rows and seen only white-skinned people, an alien world. During the day, I worked with reservation Indians who were trying to survive in the city, to get GEDs, food, jobs, rooms, any sort of survival in this America. At the party, a university affair, I stayed late and helped finish off the wine, then left with a person I'd thought of as a friend. At his home, he also drank scotch, used marijuana and cocaine. Three things I didn't know. I drank only beer and wine, mostly cheap, and in great quantities, unlike the rum and Coke, the Singapore slings of my first young years as a drunk.

After witnessing his self-destruction, knowing he was wounded by the Vietnam War, wondering how he lived through the night, I woke up the next morning in a suicidal depression so deep I called AA. I attended a Native AA group. There I discovered my problems were not confined to myself. I listened to the painful stories of other Indian people.

That was when I first began to know, really know, that history, like geography, lives in the body and it is marrow-deep. History is our illness. It is recorded there, laid down along the tracks and pathways and synapses. I was only one of the fallen in a lineage of fallen worlds and people. Those of us who walked out of genocide by some cast of fortune still struggle with the brokenness of our bodies and hearts. Terror, even now, for many of us, is remembered inside us, history present in our cells that came from our ancestor's cells, from bodies hated, removed, starved, and killed.

▲   ▲   ▲

I REMEMBER READING that after the Sand Creek Massacre, when the men returned to their camp and found their women and children killed and mutilated, even sexually mutilated, they were in such dismay and despair that they stabbed and cut themselves, taking pain into the body, away from what was seen. There was no way to send it away from the self, soul, or mind. There would always be that memory of terror. They were unable to fight the horror of the new America, the change of the world from a beautiful, loved one into the horror of devastation and the cruelty that came along with it. There was not a language, even then, for such pain. That was the reason they hurt themselves. And the distance of this history still reverberates, entering into this and every day. We are never not Indians. We have never forgotten this history.

The white men, after the massacre at Sand Creek, bragged about it on the streets of Denver. There was the white man who bought the skulls of the Sand Creek massacre victims and used them for target practice. He was the same man who captured and broke Black Kettle's famous colt that ran wild for thirteen years. This too, their human darkness, continues today. It is the darkness that makes us want to drink, the story of war and its tidal wave of violence, the falling of countries and civilizations. We human beings need to greatly reflect on what this means, the inhumanity that lives within a human, side by side with our beauty and promise.

▲   ▲   ▲

IN SPITE OF a geography changed, interrupted histories and lives, there were brilliant native leaders. Shawnee Metacomet (Tecumseh) traveled the continent, even to our tribes in the Southeast and into Florida, where he met with Osceola in order to band together into a resistance movement. Osceola hid his people in mangrove swamps for twelve years, evading the military. Multitudes of Europeans were arriving, greatly changing the land. Native languages, larger and more encompassing than English, were forbidden and changed, spiritual traditions banned. Brilliant strong leaders had no choice but to somehow endure. Sitting Bull, the man who tried to save his people, the man who said so beautifully that he was sending his heart across the miles to his homeland, found himself forced to become part of Buffalo Bill's Wild West Show.

For white Americans, even today, we Indians came to represent spirit, heart, an earth-based way of living, but the true stories of our lives were, and are still, missing from history, the geography of our lands changed. In those days, there were photographs of leaders who were dying, some propped up for the photographers and painters. While the living bodies of tribal people were destroyed, photographs and paintings romanticized Indian lives. It was, and still is, a turned-around world.

The traveling photographers created posed depictions of

people living traditional lives they no longer, in reality, by American law, were allowed to live. What comes to my mind is a portrait photograph of Charles Eastman, the Santee Sioux medical doctor. Dressed in traditional clothing, he appears to be a chief. Inside the face of the portrait is Eastman, Ohiyesa, the author and medical doctor, a survivor of wars, attending physician at the Wounded Knee massacre of Indian people, primarily women, elders, and children. He was portrayed as the brave warrior—not as the physician. He was seen as the image of what the Americans had killed but at the same time romanticized and longed for. The grief inside him was enormous.

For a time, Eastman had been in great demand as a lecturer across the country. He wrote in "The Soul of the White Man" that the new people, the Christians, did not live their "wonderful conception of exemplary living." It appeared, he said, that they were "anxious to pass on their religion to all races of men, but keep very little of it themselves. I have not seen the meek inherit the earth, or the peacemakers receive high honor." He wrote, too, that "when I let go my instinctive, nature religion, I hoped to gain something far loftier."

Instead, he finally left white America and returned to the forest of his origin. One day, back in the woodlands, as if to return him to nature, a large tortoise scratched on the door and entered the house.

Fallen: Images

EASTMAN POINTED OUT that the new kinds of people were impossible then, as now, to understand, in their duplicity. The attending physician invited the artist George Catlin to watch Osceola's death. Catlin wrote about Osceola, the brilliant, though western-educated, mixed-blood Seminole leader who kept his people hidden in the Florida swamps and Everglades for over twelve years as the United States Army searched for them. Catlin wrote that he had never met a more intelligent and genteel man. Then, after his death, Osceola's severed head was placed on the bed of the doctor's children whenever they misbehaved.

Chief Joseph's skull became an ashtray for a dentist who bought it. Our fallen worlds, our anguish, became their curiosities and souvenirs.

There was also Four Bears, a Mandan leader who wanted peace. Four Bears was painted by Catlin in his traditional clothing at the same time that he and his people were dying of smallpox the painters and photographers helped spread. The tragedy of this went unmentioned by Catlin and others. The Mandans were nearly extincted.

Yet, there was then, as now, a search by Euro-Americans for what they thought American Indians represented. Not for the best of what we have to offer, our knowledge of the world, our complex theologies, our remembered ecology, but for a romantic tie to the earth the Europeans have forgotten and severed, and could now have back, but for self-deceit. They could have what it is they want but they would have to change. Now, too, is a time of great anger, the backlash of white Americans who need to find and abide by their own integrity.

Laurens Van der Post, a white man who lived among the Bushmen of Africa, talked about what happens in a world surrounding and overwhelming indigenous peoples. He wrote of the white man's guilt as the "guilt that grows great and angry." Interestingly, he too comments that the destruction of the body and land have coincided in history. He calls it the "defoliation of landscape and spirit." It is true on this continent, too, that our world changed from one where every place and thing mattered and was loved, into a world defoliated, where nothing, human or other, mattered.

The Soul of the White Man, the Soul of the Indian

RELIGIONS HAVE SEARCHED for the location of the soul inside the human. The poet Rilke said that "what is within surrounds us." We create the world from ourselves, he means, and our perception of it. But for the Native mind, the world creates and gives birth to us and our spirits, along with all the rest. The soul resides in the world around us; it shares itself with us. We breathe its breath. We are blessed by its light.

▲   ▲   ▲

FROM A WORLD and its sacred inhabitants, rock, plant, and animal, where all was respected and loved, and in its rightful place, America has greatly changed. When the sacred animals were killed, when killers, like Buffalo Bill, became heroes, when knowledge that had evolved over tens of thousands of years was suddenly interrupted, forbidden, and untaught, the people who had believed harmony was the measure of wealth were now lost, and surrounded by a different kind of human being.

There are places where this change has been immediately clear, with no gap in time or history, such as in northern Quebec. Twenty years ago began the enormously destructive development of a hydroelectric project in James Bay, Quebec.

Many of the Cree and Inuit people were forced out of their homes without warning. The bulldozers appeared one day at their front doors, and the people were told to leave. Many lost their homes, the rivers were rerouted, their land covered and torn, their fishing camps and traplines gone. Not long after the invasion, many of the children became so self-destructive that their families had to tie their hands to keep them from committing suicide.

▲   ▲   ▲

WHEN I THINK back to the absolute pain of our histories, I understand the relief alcohol must have been on the trail where my own people cried. The whiskey sellers followed. The thieves stole what they could along the way. There were chases into Oklahoma, the theft of land, and then the land rush that took away even more Indian land, the vision of watching the death of so many buffalo and horses that the whole world seemed ruined and covered with carrion. Alcohol became a way of surviving this pain. Wagon wheel tracks eroded the earth and railroads crossed sacred ground. A new world was built on the old, and as it has turned out, the new world was, and is, lesser. Now when I go to the city, and I see my people on the streets, drunk, I don't know how anyone can wonder why it is this way. It is a hard country, with fallen hearts. These are history's body evidence.

▲   ▲   ▲

TO STOP DRINKING is an act of courage and brings with it a terrible grief. This courage is hard come by. I know strong men who cannot stop, and I can understand the mysterious deaths of Hmong men, in their sleep, when nothing is medically wrong. Pain, a doctor once told me, has only so many means of expression.

Urban Indians

THERE WAS A documentary film, *The Exiles*, made in the 1950s. The film is about the Native people who had been relocated from their reservations to Los Angeles. It is significant because there is so much unrecorded history after the massacre at Wounded Knee. *The Exiles* follows the history of the Relocation Act, which removed Indians from their reservations or allotment lands and sent them into cities. Native people were given transportation, often to the farthest cities from their homes in an attempt to break up reservation life and assimilate the people into the other America. The film is footage of Native people who had been relocated, and it shows a stark city life. The people spoke of trying to go home. The cameras, in fact, followed one man home, and it was clear, in his return, how different he was from the rest of his family. It is a bleak, tragic film. The only happy moments in it were in the night when they were all together on a hill overlooking the city, singing and drumming together. They were drinking. It made me cry to see it, because I know what follows.

The relocated were culturally in a double bind, with new and precarious beginnings. These were the times of my own beginning. Fortunately, I had my uncle, Wesley. He, with a few other people, began an organization in Denver to assist the removed, and when we went to powwows—they were always small then and held in school gyms—we would dance the wrong direction from other tribes. He knew how we Chicka-

saws danced traditionally. Hand in hand we danced. He had
the courage to do it. Nevertheless, I was young and embarrassed. I wanted to fit in. I followed the others, mostly Northern Plains tribes, until I went home to where we danced the
way he had done.

My uncle was a traditional, I see now. He spoke Chickasaw.
He knew our songs, the dances. He spoke our language and
would tell me the words, hoping I would remember.

I wish he had lived long enough to see us taking back our
lives. In history, before removal, we were the unconquerable.
We were warriors who split off from the more peaceful people. We were named the "They Left Not a Great While Ago"
people.

I wish I could take this uncle home for a Stomp Dance
where the old people cry with gratitude that our old ways continued in spite of having been forbidden and dangerous. I sit
and watch the men put water on the ground for our dancing.
I know we are back. Some of us cry when we dance. Old men
and women, with the young. Dancing around the fire. Belong-
ing.

▲ ▲ ▲

FALLING ISN'T ALWAYS bad. Sometimes it is into a better
world. When I think of my drunken falls, it was as if I wanted
to fall into my own life, fall to the healing earth. My instinct
had been right, my way wrong. Sometimes now, for the sheer
joy of it, I roll in the grasses where my horses have rolled while
they watch, or I smell the odor of earth and remember a story
of how the mud mother shaped her little ones, the humans,
and held them in her lap. She rocked them, those red clay
children with their tiny fingers, their smooth faces. She rocked

them and swayed. The wind came to breathe life into them. That first aliveness, that first gust of air inside the clay people, brought them to life. The mud mother loved her children. She sang and spoke strong words to them, Oh bodies, oh infants, our future, my children, flesh of the earth.

And those children down on earth, just created from there, sometimes now have powerful voices and have survived.

SILENCE IS MY MOTHER

I

Solitude; my mother, tell me my life.
— CZESLAW MILOSZ

Daughters

I SIT NOW in a chair in their room, silent, and look out the window at the hills and mountains I wake to each day. In my hand, the first pictures of my daughters. They are wearing fancy dresses, one red, one peach. It was twenty-one years ago today that they arrived, and in the pictures they look washed, combed, soft.

I first saw my adopted daughters in another photograph taken by the adoption worker. My younger, Jeanette, sat on a car outside a fast food restaurant. She wore a dark brown coat and a fierce-eyed anger, but looked as if, given the right conditions, she might smile.

She was a tiny five-year-old girl with a stubborn streak, but a hint of sweetness. She was a wisp of a child with thick long black hair falling down her back, as if all her bodily energy had grown into hair instead of bone and flesh, for she was mal-nourished, weighed only twenty-four pounds, and was silent. Her teeth had all decayed and were capped with aluminum. Under her eyes were dark circles, a trait I later learned to recognize in many abused children, as if they never sleep, are always vigilant.

In the same photograph my older daughter, Marie, stood nearby, her back against the building, her eyes unfocused. She was a ten-year-old girl filled with silent rage and horrible pain, one who looked through things and people, not at them. In a worn blue coat, she gazed off into the distance beyond the camera, toward a past and not a future. Her fine hair had a red light in it, and her face was beautiful already and full, almost womanly at the age of ten. The faraway look, we thought at the time, was because of the change she was having to make, moving into a house with strangers she had met only five or six times before, strangers who would become her mother and father, strangers who had large expectations, hopes, and dreams for her and for themselves. She was a child who had no say in the matter, no control over what was to become of her. Later, when her history began to unfold, her entry here, into this home, this room I sit in, was insignificant for her; she was already broken and wounded beyond what could be repaired.

She was already a child who'd lost her core. She had no conscience, no reference points outside herself, and was violent. Twenty years later I still wonder how such ice exists in a human. I still fear it. I still can hardly speak it. I wonder, also, how, in my wish for love, I came to stand beside it. Once in a while Marie would say or do something that gave me a measure of hope. Each time, I held to it a bit longer than I should have.

The girls were clearly uncared-for, their county records lost. On our first visits to the foster home, the foster mother had been angry that we had given gifts to the girls but nothing to her "own." She tried to keep the stuffed animals we gave them at our first visit. One was a mother kangaroo with a baby in her pouch, the other a mother monkey with an infant's arms wrapped around it, clinging with the strength of Velcro, in what looked like love.

The clothes the girls wore in the photographs taken by the adoption agency, the red and peach dresses, were kept by the foster family for their "own" children. "Own." A word of possession, one that separates out chosen children in a world too small for love, with people too cruel for warmth. They had even kept the Halloween candy the girls had been given the October before, and given it to their "own." I marvel over the smallness on which they built their lives. And yet I suppose their lives too had been destroyed, ravaged by some history unknown to me.

That their foster mother tried to keep the animals for her own children was still another indication of how askew things had gone, and the fact that she was not even aware of its visibility should have been a warning. The foster home was a place devastated, with torn-up linoleum covered with filth, furniture carved with a knife and broken, odors of garbage mingled with human smells.

The foster mother disliked us, not because she cared for the children, and we were taking them away, but because of what we might learn of her. She was a woman who couldn't read or write, and so had no power herself, a poor woman who lived with a violent man. The children were her income. When we left the last time, to bring the girls to this home where I now sit, she said, in their presence, "You can keep that one. She's evil. But the older girl can come back." She, the girl who had been the woman's baby-sitter and house-cleaner, who'd rarely been allowed to attend school, and was the sexual victim of her husband, a police officer in a small town.

Ironically, Jeanette, the younger one, the unwanted one, was the one who survived. She had been given away to the foster grandmother, who was lonely. Later, she told of being locked frequently in a dark basement. Her coat was once pinned on the clothesline above the barking dog she feared and she was forced to retrieve it. There was only one person who had been kind to her, the grandfather, who had died.

After the placement of the girls into our home, the next time we visited, as part of the adoption process, the family had moved. In their new home everything was new. Their three children each had their own rooms, stereos, clothing, new bikes, new furniture. Even though they were young, my daughters and I discussed often how this drastic change had come about. It is still a mystery. Did they hoard the foster care money? We didn't know.

▲　　　▲　　　▲

THERE WAS NO history of the girls' lives to come along with them. There were no other photographs of them as children, no stories passed down to them, no stories about their first words or their first steps. No one who loved them. They were beginning a life with us already wounded, born into their new life fully created at the ages of five and ten. They came from a world of many silences. Even their new birth certificates had been altered to say they were born of my body, as if their lives began only with us, the past a territory of lies and silences.

Rainstorm

IT WAS AN unsteady May. The rainy day they arrived, the windows were fogged over, the earth saturated with water. I ran to the car, a newspaper over my head. My husband already sat behind the wheel, the windshield wipers moving.

When we arrived at the foster home, things were in dissarray, the foster mother angry. They gave us a cardboard box. Inside the box was a worn-out woman's swimsuit, a woman's sleeveless shirt, and a broken blue-eyed doll whose eyes closed and opened, as if it could see what it wanted and not the rest. It was as if the mother had picked the contents haphazardly, giving them anything she didn't want. The girls did not arrive at our home with dignity, but with the debris of other lives, in all ways. Nor did it seem as if they'd miss them. In all those years, no love had grown between the girls and their foster families.

I felt a growing rage as I learned the fragmented stories of the broken children; there was also a sudden coldness and danger in the world as I saw it through their lives. Still, sometimes even now I search through phone books for their foster parents when I travel to different cities. To do what, I don't know. Surely not to talk to them. Not to see them, either. I suppose it is to keep in place the force of evil, to identify it and, in so doing, not to have to fear it.

▲   ▲   ▲

THE DAY THE girls came to live with us, my happiness was great. That day, on the drive home, they both sat in the back-seat. I was anxious with the excitement of our new life as par-ents. Now and then I looked in the mirror to see their reflections. Jeanette was a tiny unwashed girl with a long mane of dark hair and an angry, stubborn set to her mouth. Marie's eyes were wide open, unblinking, as if in shock, like a person asleep. We knew the move would be difficult. We didn't know how much they'd already been traumatized. Our first meetings with the girls had been in offices and restaurants. We'd learned only a small part of their histories from the county and the agency. The rest would unfold slowly, over time.

▲   ▲   ▲

AND SO, ON a rainy day, they arrived with their box of debris, two daughters born to the same birth mother and with different fathers, one father murdered in front of the older girl, one whose whereabouts were unknown, as was his paternity uncertain. It is just that life, the birth of these two beautiful children, takes its risks and chances to enter where it will, where it can. Now they had a destiny with us, my husband and me, and we had a destiny with them.

Heavy rain fell on the house, the windows, the earth. It rained ceaselessly. Our house is built into a hillside. It was made in the 1940s of salvaged war materials, and it seemed the house would wash down to the canyon bottom. Mud splashed up from the road, snakes left their dens for higher ground, and the alarmed birds of spring called out. The nearby creek was rushing down overfilled and muddy. On the battery-operated radio, we listened to the news about the storm. People were being rescued from hillsides by helicopter. The dam above us was watched carefully, sandbags placed above this little town that was once ruined by flood. A transformer on a nearby utilities pole was struck by lightning and exploded with a sound and flash of light, as if a bomb had gone off. But, with all this noise, in our home there were no voices, no words from the girls. There were only silences. Our house, which had seemed to us so happy to be having children, was now a leaking container of pain, silence, and sleeplessness. One girl continued to stare into space. The other retreated into herself, so very small, huddling. But at night they came alive and walked around the room, creaking the floors.

Years before we adopted the girls, while Christmas shopping, my husband and I went out for lunch. At the restaurant, I saw mothers and daughters sitting together, talking over food. Suddenly I wished I'd had that kind of relationship in my life. I overheard them talking about their personal lives and I felt a sense of loss. I hadn't seen mother-and-daughter relationships before. It was as if it had taken this many years to even recognize what I'd missed. I remember thinking that since I had never had this kind of relationship with my own mother, then I'd one day become that kind of mother, nurturing, friendly, with a daughter, maybe two.

That same evening, as we were driving home in a light snow, we passed a street of bars. I watched from the car window as a woman put a child into a cab in front of a bar. I believe she said she couldn't pay the driver. When Marie arrived, I seemed to recall that this was this same child. Some days I am sure of it, that it was a moment of fate, our being there at that precise moment, that she would later become our own child. In my mind, somewhere, real or imagined, the picture of that child being sent away in the cab became one and the same as my older adopted daughter.

When we decided we wanted children, adoption was our way of family-making. We wanted children already in the world and without homes. We first learned of the girls because I worked at the Native American center. The Indian Child Welfare Act went into effect that year, 1978, allowing Indian families to adopt children of the same tribe, or, if no family in a child's tribe was available, another tribe. At the time, in our region alone, there were six hundred American Indian children in foster care homes, needing Indian families. Suddenly, in a turn of the law, we were considered a first choice for the placement of children from our own communities.

Within five months we were the parents of these two daughters, on that day surrounded by rain and storm. They had fear. They found themselves suddenly in a new place, with red mud running down the road and lightning cracking the sky. Even though they were silent, I tried to talk with them. I sat with them thinking how much they needed to be loved, washed, and fed, how hidden their beauty. I didn't know that our relationship was wronged by something beyond my ken.

▲　　　▲　　　▲

NOW, OVER TWENTY years later, at the sunny window of what was once their room, I feel I can almost touch them, smell them. I look back to the rainy day they arrived, and I see them, as if they were here. The storm that day announced that my illusions about love, family, and children were about to be washed away. I had always believed in the power of love to heal. Love, I believed, was a mighty force. What I didn't know was that it isn't always enough. Instead there was devastation and changes never foreseen. The day the girls moved in, the red earth road along which we lived was almost washed away, as if to signify that we were beginning something that had no trail into it, and no road out. It was an irrevocable act, adoption, a thing of potential, for both heartbreak and love. There would be no return, ever, to what we had been before, as people, alone and together.

Until then, what I thought of as love was as immature and unwise as I was. I know now that it is like time; it grows as time passes. It doesn't always make for betterment. It always requires growth.

I believed I could help fill young hearts with love and so transform them. Still, I can see, there is something to it, to love, that is. I watch my younger daughter now. Years later, she is a kind and patient mother.

▲   ▲   ▲

IN TIME, THE story of my daughters unfolded, facts revealed only little by little. As with a photographic print, the pictures floated slowly into being. Marie was a girl violated and tortured. She had lived through horrors most of us could not imagine. She had been abused, even as an infant, burned by cigarettes and hot wires, and raped. She was a girl who was once dropped off by her mother and her mother's boyfriend on a dark country road in their attempt to lose her. Somehow she survived. That night, pushed out of the car, she found her way back. But she never found her way back to herself as a child, the one that existed before the violence, the child that might have been. So when, years later, she said of her own daughter, "This isn't my daughter. My child died," she meant, without intending it, the loss of her own self. She would never return. She is yet, over twenty years later, still a tangle of threads and war-torn American Indian history that other Americans like to forget. Her story is not yet fully deciphered. Perhaps it will never be, nor will it end. Inside remains a knot that isn't of her own tying, a painful world not of her own making. She had grown up in the silence of records and courts, words and letters and memos of other people's making.

But even more than that, she is the result of a shattered world. She came from the near obliteration of a people. In retrospect, after years of thought on our lives, I realize that we had entered, and taken in, a war that was more than child abuse or the lack of love. Along with the girls, history came to live with us, the undeniable, unforgotten aspect of every American Indian life. She was a remnant of American history, and the fires of a brutal history had come to bear on her. As a Lakota girl, with her large eyes that looked not at anything, she was the result of Custer's dream, containing the American violences, the people from another continent, that entered this land without compassion.

▲   ▲   ▲

ONE NIGHT, AT a traditional dance and powwow, when the girls were still young, a woman I was certain was their birth mother stood up and in a sorrowfully drunken voice spoke into the microphone, telling about herself, the many children she'd lost, the drunkenness of her life. As she wept, I felt so much compassion for her, for this woman who had lost so much and now stood there so small in front of us all. The other people in the auditorium seemed uncomfortable hearing her, having to confront this illness that has been given over to us by our histories as Indian people. I wanted to go to the woman who embodied the plight of so many of us, to hold her, to show her the girls. But I couldn't. I knew what it would mean. I knew how broken she was. I knew, also, that even though violent and damaged, she was a woman who had come from beautiful people, warriors, healers, and those who had been dreamers. She, in her very being, was the consequence, the near end, of our Indian dreaming on this continent.

Ohiyesa

"I WANT TO tell you my story." This is what Indian people say. And our stories do not begin with us as individuals. The story of my daughters began a hundred years ago.

I try to think about what it means, the bodily hatred that would loose itself on a child in the form of torture, so purposefully cold and with intent to harm. It is a coldness that has its origins in events, not people. In this case, I go back to the Massacre at Wounded Knee. I look back and see what forces led to the twisted violence, to the hatred of a mother's self and the beautiful children born of her body. The story of my daughters and their birth mother calls to mind this historical massacre and a man named Charles Eastman. That's his American name. Ohiyesa was his real name. He was a Santee Sioux medical doctor and a writer of the late nineteenth century. His boyhood was one of traditional indigenous living. His father was one of the starving people who, after an uprising against the U.S. government, were captured and removed to stockades and camps. One day, years later, his father returned and decided that Ohiyesa should learn about European-

American culture. And so, as an adult, Eastman was a western-trained medical doctor who graduated from Dartmouth. His contributions as a medical doctor and as a writer would have been significant in any time, but they were especially so in that time. He was the medical doctor at the Pine Ridge Reservation, where my daughters come from. After the Wounded Knee Massacre, Ohiyesa, on his horse, led a search party through the drifts and mounds of snow that had fallen over frozen bodies, to see if there were survivors who'd escaped. In their search, they found an old blind woman still alive, and a baby girl who had been shielded by her mother's body. He was the one who witnessed firsthand the massacres, dismemberment, and mutilation of the people, and he was the one who tried to heal the survivors.

I have always wondered what were the effects of the massacre on him, the healer. Ohiyesa is one of the named people in this part of history that I care about, though from my daughters' origin there are many others. One is Sitting Bull, who worked so profoundly to save and settle his people in the north, away from the Americans. He was tricked and killed shortly before the massacre. There was also the elusive, unphotographed Crazy Horse, who was dedicated to his own band of people, the group from which my younger daughter descended.

Few people outside our cultures can comprehend the depth of the pain, despair, and, for many of us Native peoples, anger. To other Americans, this history, if thought of at all, belongs to a far past, but in truth these events are recent and remembered. We have not forgotten the past so quickly and easily. For me, I love the men and women who fought, even knowing as they did that it was an unwinnable fight.

Susto: Soul Loss

AND SO, COMING out of history, emerging from these old wars, here were living girls, the legacy of that history. The girls had been abandoned in Denver by their birth mother. Until a neighbor noticed them, the oldest had gone through trash in the alley to find food for herself and her infant sister. Her life, at six years old, had already been a nightmare, and she was a child who had to leave it, if only in spirit, mind, or heart. As a mother I would be brought up short against any illusions or expectations I might have had about our future together. I was forced to face the Native history that had been at work in their lives and pasts.

From out of history, it would all come to rest in my home and my heart.

▲   ▲   ▲

A HEALER, A curandera, who works at a clinic in Denver speaks about soul loss. *Susto*, she calls it, and "soul loss" is the closest term I can think of to describe the condition of children who have been so deeply damaged. There are many versions and notions of soul loss, in all traditions. In an intelligent essay by Gerald Vizenor in his book *The People Named the Chippewa*, he writes about a grandmother who killed her grandchild because she believed the child was evil and possessed by malevolent forces. Even as she held pillows over his face, she said, "It was like he could breathe right through the pillows." She took the child to the hospital. "When the medical doctor uncovered the child he found two ceremonial willow sticks in his chest." These were Sun Dance stakes.

The grandmother, who had operated out of fear, was committed to a mental hospital. She was convinced the child was the "spawn of the devil," and no one could argue with her. She had even felt that there was "something" in the house. And she believed she was rescuing her grandson by smothering him. There is something inexplicable and horrifying about such an event. Now, however, children who cause fear in adults are called unattached, or unbonded.

In a recent article in the *New York Times* about the unattached children from Eastern Europe who have been adopted by American families, one of the adoptive mothers says, "There are times when I felt I was getting the soul back." She describes her child, a girl of five who didn't have cause-and-effect thinking, didn't know that plants were alive but furniture wasn't. Another child, the article says, would stiffen and try to get away from her adoptive mother.

Children who have not bonded will do anything to remain unbonded. Intimacy is the greatest threat. They dissociate, and because they don't acknowledge others are alive, they are prone to violence.

I came from another time, a different background, from the woman who killed the child, but with our oldest, I, too, felt we were dealing with something beyond us, something fearsome, as if we'd been taken on a journey to the underworld. Looking back, I now reflect on Cree stories of Windigo and other monsters who had hearts of ice, hearts that had to be melted for the person's survival. At the western edge are stories of feral children, those who could not survive in the world of humans. I believe these, too, are the stories of those who, like our daughters, were unbonded and uncared for. For such a child, love is the greatest threat and human closeness is a danger to the life force itself.

Early in the adoption process, we'd seen films of children

who were unbonded. They had a fierceness. Their behaviors were unfathomable to most. There was one child, Amber, who had torn up a rug and shredded it with her own small hands, one boy who tore an entire wall apart with only his fingers. Before our own adoption, the stories other parents told were unlike anything we could imagine. We didn't entirely believe them. Like illness and other tragedies, these things happened only to others. We were sure of ourselves and unrealistic.

My former husband, who has taken strongly to Christianity in recent years, said he now believes that we were in the presence of something he can't account for with his faith or belief. Nothing in his logical mind could ever contain or make sense of the events around the girls, their behavior, their pain, the way their disturbance, present and palpable, carried into the house. It did seem that we were in the grip of something unnamed. Though I shy away from this word, we were in the presence of a kind of evil. Evil is utterly banal, as writer Hannah Arendt said about the holocaust in Europe, and it is ordinary. It comes from so small a thing as records misplaced or poorly written, from mothers who hate themselves and thus their offspring, from people overwhelmed by jobs and lives and histories, even from those people who don't speak up against injustice.

Feral Children

IT IS HARD, almost impossible, to hold as true that there are children who will only drink from a toilet, refuse to eat, tear carpets into pieces with their bare hands, or, like my daughter, torture the family dog. Feral, some might have said in the past.

And perhaps, in history, this has been true. I've read accounts of children found who were not raised by human mothers, but by wolves. The wolf children grew up in worlds not of human making. At the approach of humans they showed their teeth or attempted to scratch or bite. Even their eyes, one person said, perhaps exaggerating, had a peculiar blue glare in the darkness of night, and could see what others can't.

But wolf parents, at least, did not injure their human children. A visiting bishop said of the wolf girl Kamala, a year after her life with humans began, "She was a very sweet child when spoken to . . . but if she were left alone, she would retire to the darkest corner, crouch down, and remain with her face to the wall. . . ." Two years later he visited again and he noted that while the wolves had not been able to teach anything especially human to their little human cubs, they "had not taught them anything bad." The children had no vices. Kamala died shortly thereafter, being used as both a specimen and a curiosity.

The Silent Daughter

IT IS THE young, silent girl I talk about now, the one we thought shy. We didn't know, at first, that she didn't speak. Her sister always spoke for her. For a time after she moved into this room where I sit, she was afraid to let go of me. At five years of age, she weighed only twenty-four pounds and was like an infant. For the first summer months, thin as a spider, she held on to me, clinging fiercely. Once, on a sunny spring day, we had a picnic in the park. After I read her a book, she napped. The day was hot, we were both sweating, so I loosened her grip and moved away from her slightly. She woke, afraid, grasping me around the middle. I gave in and let her cling. For several months I carried her like a possum mother, attached to my body.

I was thrilled by this at first, thinking that she desperately needed love. I affectionately called her a spider monkey, but as paradoxical as it seems, she soon changed and was first diagnosed as "unattached," a girl like the one on the films from the adoption agency. Soon, like other unattached children, she would go to strangers and embrace them. They thought her an endearing child. At home, she would seldom sleep and would hurt herself. This lovely child was holding on to everyone in the same way she had done with me, strangers she had never met, men who were dazzled by her attention, were charmed by the small wisp of a girl with a black waterfall of hair falling down her back, making it even more difficult when we dragged her, screaming, away from them, making them want to be her rescuers. It was the "indiscriminate affection" spoken of in a *New York Times Magazine* article on unattached children.

At home, she became a terror to us. She hardly slept. She hurt herself, this child who couldn't speak.

With our oldest daughter, all the pain fell outward, onto others, whom she would hit or abuse, but for Jeanette, pain came to an inward point.

Usually it took both of us to hold her down. At times, growing exhausted, we worked in shifts as she tried furiously to kick and bite. When we carried her through a door, she would put her arms in the doorway to keep from passing through, a move that might have broken her arms. We thought maybe she had a mote of trust, a particle of faith that we wouldn't hurt her, but in truth, she didn't care about broken bones or pain.

To our good fortune, we lived only a town away from the center that specializes in attachment disorders in adopted and foster children. It is the place where they practice something called Z therapy, because it is a last resort. It consists of holding and frustrating the children into reactions, then soothing them. This is the same place where the adoptive parents of children from Eastern Europe are taking their children now, children with many of the same behaviors and traits as our beautiful daughters, but from neglect and lack of physical contact more than from abuse.

A woman in a nearby town was convicted of child abuse, but claimed that her adopted son, unattached, had beaten himself to death with a wooden spoon. No one believed her. How could anyone? It is so foreign to imagine a child beating himself. And yet I've seen it.

There was another child in Colorado Springs, one who was accustomed to getting up in the night to hurt himself. He was strapped to his bed and died one night from his own vomit. The parents were arrested for abuse and neglect even though hundreds of letters from mental health professionals supported the parents and told how and why this had happened, explaining that the straps were to keep the boy safe from his own self-violence.

▲   ▲   ▲

AT THE TREATMENT center, the children would be held, irritated, tickled, whatever it took to put them into a rage or an emotional explosion. When they reached that point, they would then be cared for, held and loved. The purpose was to restore the filaments of relationship to them, the bonding that should have taken place in the early years of a child's development. At the time, hearing our younger daughter cry out behind the closed doors of the office, I thought it abusive. I wanted to get her and leave. But by then I knew there would be no hope for her if this therapy didn't work. It was because of this then controversial therapy that Jeanette talked for the first time. She came out of the office on the second day and, ending her long silence, said, "Would you come in now?" All five words. Crying, my husband and I stood and followed this miracle child into the office of the woman we still call our savior.

Holding. The word means so much.

▲   ▲   ▲

IN REAL LIFE, hearts break and sometimes remain that way, things and people close and never open again. As a mother, I thought love could make up for history, theirs and mine. My visions of our future had been happy ones, but truth was something else. Still, there was no turning back. Also, there was no way to return to being the persons we were "before," that magic word of our lives, measurements significant, made and weighed daily, breath by breath. We were changed irrevocably into new people.

Lost Souls, Stolen Children

"I THINK IT was their business, taking souls," said Inupiat Florence Kenney in an interview with Jane Katz. She speaks of the tragic legacy of Indian boarding schools. The boarding schools created many of the troubles we still have in our communities today. "School separated us; I hardly ever saw my little sister or brothers. We forgot our language," she says. "We were called numbers. I was Miss 14."

"The loneliness was so deep I froze," says Ramona Bennett, former Pullayup tribal chair. She speaks about the difficulties of not learning humanity or love in the boarding schools. "You don't get a chance to know human beings, to see them laugh as well as cry."

▲   ▲   ▲

AND ZITKALA SA, the turn-of-the-century Lakota writer, wrote of her own experience, of weeping with no mother or aunts to wipe her tears, of huddling in corners, crawling under the bed. "And no one came to comfort me. Not a soul reasoned quietly with me, as my mother used to do; for now I was only one of many little animals driven by a herder."

Many other American Indian writers told of this experience, from contemporary poet Mary Tall Mountain to Pretty Shield. I remember once hearing a man telling, and still crying, about how as a boy he and his brother reached for each other as they were forced apart, into different schools, the bond purposely broken in order for the children to be assimilated into American ways of being.

And when the children returned, their families often did not recognize or know them. They looked, dressed, and spoke like the ones who had stolen them. The children thought in smaller ways, too, having lost the great tracts of knowledge and ways of being contained in their own languages, the words that came from living on and with a land. Most of the stolen said they were not able to go back home, to wholly go back, so it became a tragedy in many parts, some of it still with us today.

With generations, often two or more, of children sent away

and stolen in this manner, who of them learned how to be a mother or father? All of this is passed on to ourselves and to my daughters, in a chain of history, the links of which we are now trying to break apart.

Failures

OUR SEARCH FOR doctors that might help Marie, our older daughter, seemed fruitless. Most therapists couldn't, didn't, grasp the extent of the damage done to her. Her problems showed up later, and by then the county no longer approved Z therapy, and so we were on our own, looking for other sources of help. It was as if, like us, the therapists couldn't let themselves believe, let alone admit, that they were powerless over damaged children. Ordinary talk therapy and analysis are not operative when a child is in this realm of pain. Nor were medications. Early on, when we first brought the girls home, one doctor I called said they should be hospitalized, but the county and the adoption agency both said it would disrupt their bonding in our home. No one seemed to have a sense of the gravity of our situation. One well-dressed social worker explained her tan by saying she had just been to Mexico on vacation. Her advice was to put a list of chores on the refrigerator door for the girls to complete and to go into family therapy. We could only laugh at the absurdity. We had a violent child who fed needles to the dog, who had physically attacked me in the car as I drove, who heard voices and spoke to them, who left feces on the kitchen table and broke windows. Nothing, no one, was more removed from what was happening, from reality, than the county employees with whom we had contact. And unbelievably, even though the foster family was known to be abusive, one county continued to place children with them. It was decided they were unfit for older children but could still have infants.

The county referred us to another center for Marie than the one that helped Jeanette. There, talking to the doctor one day, I said Marie had defecated on the table. The doctor asked if it was solid. I looked at her with dismay. I knew in that moment she would be unable to help us.

None of the other families who'd been in our adoption support group survived that first year. None still had their children. They were heartbroken, and felt like failures because their adoptions had not worked. Their children, once again, were moved, and everyone lost. They were left with the feeling, for the rest of their lives, that they were inadequate. Ironically, it was out of their capacity for love that they had become another part of the pain of the children. In particular, I remember a nurse and her husband who had adopted a girl with leukemia and her brother. This woman's son kicked the dog to death. This, I must point out, is not the typical experience of adoptive parents, but these were children who had no caregivers, who had been badly abused, who had gone already from one foster home to another.

▲   ▲   ▲

MARIE GREW UP to be a girl who would later severely abuse her own children, who would lose them, eventually, to an adoptive family. But for each of them, they'd been with her too long. Because when the unattached become mothers, all hell—even if you don't believe in it—breaks loose. It lets go its hold in the underworld and comes to the surface.

She had the logic of damaged people. One night, frustrated and angry that her new infant wouldn't walk, she locked herself and the child inside the bedroom and yelled at her while we stood at the door, trying to jimmy the lock, fearing for the baby's life. Another time she asked me what was wrong with child pornography. It seemed to her a reasonable way to earn a living and feed a child. At the time, she resided with a man in his sixties who took in girls who were in trouble. To help them, he said, and he told me that Marie was the worst. He couldn't bring her around. He offered me the details. She heard voices. She changed personality. She was violent. He had one positive characteristic: he was worried about Marie's new baby.

Marie had already said, in a straightforward manner, that she would hurt her own daughter, and later her son. The county employees already knew Marie by the time her son was born, and they were present at the beginning of her son's life. Even so, he went into two foster homes before finding his way, fortunately, to the family that had adopted her daughter.

All I knew from the time Marie's man friend had called me was that I had to do everything to keep the infant safe. I called the Kemp Center on Child Abuse, because the county was of no help. To the county workers, Marie seemed sane in her presentation of herself. It was a capability—to seem sane—that never helped her. The county workers seemed to think, instead, that I was meddling until Marie threw a lamp at the crying infant, threatened to kill her, and then threw a Christmas tree. It was the older man, finally, who turned her in. And Marie told them, not only me, that her real baby had died at birth. And I suppose it is true; she meant herself, her real baby, had died.

And now, not so many years later, she has had another, her fourth.

▲   ▲   ▲

THERE WERE, AND are, silences all around my daughters, lost records, a girl who never slept, one who woke struggling and fighting, as if we might hurt her. And, as if the memory of the mother is inherited by the child, my granddaughter also sometimes wakes this way, fighting, as if such a thing is learned, and remembered by the body, even if unspoken in words. It is as if the stories of the mothers are written into the child's beginnings.

I thought so, also, with my own mother.

Searching for My Mother

MY FATHER ONCE worked in the dairy at a children's home, and I liked to ride in his aqua-and-white Chevy and accompany him to work. It was a warm place, full with the smell of cattle, cream, and straw. The presence of the milk cows was a comfort to me, as was the warm light and the smell of moisture. A family of cats lived there in the animal body heat of milk cows, the coziness of the well-kept barn. They were voiceless. Whenever I approached the mother and her kittens, they opened their mouths to speak, but no sound came out. In the warmth that provided mother's milk, they were mute and precious.

The silent kittens at the orphanage had inherited their mother's muteness. Whether it was a physical condition or whether they'd learned soundlessness, I don't know. I only know that silence, muteness, was not entirely foreign to me. Like the kittens, like my younger daughter, I first grew into my remembered life in a house without words, and as a child, I became wordless outside of home.

▲   ▲   ▲

THIS IS HOW I remember childhood, not necessarily how it was: It was in Denver. The kitchen had red trim. It was a house of four small quiet rooms. Two were bedrooms. The house itself had no interior doors, so there were no physical boundaries between my mother, my sister, and myself. There was nothing that could be opened or closed. Yet there were walls of silence between us, and silences within those that dated back how many generations I can't imagine. Silence didn't figure richly into our lives, but poorly. It wasn't the kind of quiet I would later value as that place of human regeneration and peace. It was a powerless silence.

There were wars. Japan. China. Korea. It was a time when children did not know their fathers. Like the families around us, we were a family of females. My father, a soldier, was absent, as were most of the men of those days. When he returned, so much later, to the front door, he knocked, as if he'd been gone so long and been so far away it was no longer his house. I didn't recognize him. On discovering he was not my uncle James, who looked like him and who had often visited us, I ran away and cried.

When my father was in Japan, my mother was young, and raising two daughters. She called the army and the Red Cross because our payments from the army hadn't arrived. To feed us, she ironed other people's clothes, men's white shirts, pilot's suits, and military uniforms. She stood long hours, starching clothes in a metal tub or the sink, then sprinkling them from a soda bottle with a stopper of holes. She ironed as if our lives could be so easily smoothed or creased, her legs, even young, hurting from swollen veins.

The scorch print of the iron on a shirt meant a financial loss for her, and so we had to be quiet and leave her alone, "lest" she scorch a shirt. Her family spoke this way. As if from an earlier time and language. A person "commenced" and cried, and "'twas" a good day. They were from a Pennsylvania Dutch background.

My sister tells me that my father's girlfriend in Japan wrote us letters, inquiring about our health and happiness. It was not unusual for young men away from their wives to have taken lovers. She says a long fight ensued when my father returned. I don't remember it. I was too young. It was the last fight we ever heard or saw. It was, at least in my memory, almost the last words my mother and father ever spoke to one another in our presence for many years. Now and then I'd hear them talking at night, and it was both a surprise and a comfort to me that they spoke in their bedroom. I wanted to know what they said, if decisions were being made, if they talked about us, if they said kind things to each other.

After my father's return from Japan, and that first fight, there was never an argument. This was a hurt and anger that lasted nearly forty years. She would bring it all up again if we listened too much to our father and his stories. She reminded us that he drank, that he'd been hospitalized for a year with cirrhosis. She wanted us to know he was imperfect. And though I knew he had harmed her, he became, over time, a person who had a capacity for love. Her own love developed later and was especially significant after I was in an accident, when she came to help care for me. But then, as a young mother, a woman in silence and emotional pain, she was for a time a closed door that nothing could pass through, and I remember how it began in the house with no real interior doors.

In that first doorless house of my memory, even the closets had curtains. I would sit on one end of the bed and shake the curtains as if they were the reins of my horse, and ride away. I was a cowgirl. I'd imprinted on cowboys, the men of our family, those who could fix anything but broken hearts. Even now a man with bowlegs and Wranglers will get a second look from me.

As a small child, I had a need to know my mother, and her story was something I sought. In that house and others, though I was very young, I searched for her even while she was present. I recall sitting on the floor of my mother's closet, smelling the odor of damp wall plaster mixed with the perfume she wore. I touched the fabric of her clothing, which seemed so womanly to me. On the floor were her neatly kept 1940s shoes with their round open toes and stacked heels. I tried them on and they were too big.

I hid beneath tables and watched her. I concealed myself in corners and looked out, trying to know her. I created her inside my girl's mind. I know now that every life is a knot of stories to be either untied or left tangled. Every life has stories mistold, stories approached watchfully, stories never finished, and truths of its own, hidden even from ourselves. Few of us are who we claim to be, or think we are, in act or deed or words. This, however, is only a thought and not what is in my heart, and it was my heart that wanted to learn her life, and through it, my own. My mother laid no claim, even to herself. I think she was a victim of brain chemistry in a time when there were no medications. She wanted to be invisible, inaudible. She was fearful. Every person's sight that rested on her was one of danger or judgment. I was the daughter who inherited my mother's pain and her fears. Now I know her only because I study her from inside myself, and my own inner world of fear.

▲   ▲   ▲

DURING THE WARS, my young mother, alone, was plagued by her own fears, mysterious in their origin. Perhaps it is the sad story of that generation, before medications, before the talking cure was widespread. There was a great silence around her, of what I think to be her own history, perhaps of abuse or injury, contained in her skin. Whatever it was, she was wounded, and because of the times, did not, could not, heal. And I know that we are all as much mysteries to ourselves as we are to one another. The puzzles of human minds and hearts are not easily deciphered.

When I was a young person, my loss was that, as with my daughters, I could never know her. Even now, I must create her story from pieces. The stories come only from out of myself the way a spider creates the strongest of webs from its own abdomen. That web is at once a sheltering place, a trap, and a place of beginning journeys. Something shakes it and the spider works its way toward it. Only its feet know which lines are safe to walk.

I searched for my mother in photographs and greeting cards

that were saved in the large, leather-bound family Bible. Later, I opened her bureau drawers, looking for clues to her life, and finding them, as if they would shape my own world. Unlike my own drawers, even now, hers have always been orderly, never overfilled or rummaged through in a great hurry to find something and rush away. There was no place she was going in such a threatening world as hers was, a world where someone, everyone, would hurt her, stare at her, or steal from her. But as for my sister and me, we were never still long enough to take such care with our possessions. We feared such stillness.

In one of her drawers was the black stone necklace, bracelet, and earring set my father had sent her from Japan, tucked away in a box. I thought it was beautiful. I don't know that she ever wore it. She always saved good things for the future, for "someday," for special occasions or better times, and so in the drawer it remained. And what I found there in the drawers and closets was all I knew of the woman I lived with, who birthed me.

▲   ▲   ▲

MY SISTER SAYS our mother lived in the shadow of our father. Men in that generation cast a large shadow, it is true, but certain kinds of silence don't need something or someone to stand above them and cast them into darkness.

▲   ▲   ▲

THERE WAS A field across from the silent house, and a dump beside the field which was my favorite playground. It was where we played. We salvaged things others had tossed away, going through the wreckage, trash, and rusted cars, as always, searching for something of value or use.

The inner walls sweated and ran with moisture. I was quiet. I traced the tracks of water down walls, making a place for water to follow, opening a path for it to fall, as if making a road. I noticed the minute and small, looking around me at the textures, the walls, making a tent, even indoors, to shield myself, and studying the light. Mine was a child's unhappiness, and no one was there to notice. My mother hid from doorbells, knocks, and phone calls, as if we, too, were in a war-torn world during that time of air raid sirens, drills, and fear.

We were an army family, and books and papers would come to our door, as if we were the chosen, privy to information the general public could not have, as if only soldiers' families were granted salvation. They told us what to do in case of an atomic bomb: Wash our clothing, bathe, drink boiled water. It was a world out of touch with its own capacities for harm and for evil.

▲　　　▲　　　▲

AND IN GRADE school, where we had air raid drills, my teachers would comb my hair in the mornings. They sent notes home saying I was a nervous child, asking if everything was all right. Inheriting my mother's fears, I was a child who cried, hid, escaped, whose entire energy seemed pulled between a need to disappear from others and a human desire for love. I feared airplanes and ran for cover when they passed over. The notes home, I think, must have gone unanswered. My mother was silent, not from malice but from the simple fact she was exhausted. She stayed up at night ironing. She cooked for us and cleaned. Tired, young, overwhelmed with her own life, and afraid of the world, she did her level best.

The Birthday Party

THERE ARE EVENTS or times remaining from childhood that stay with a person for no known reason, as if they wait within a person for a kind of clarity or meaning. Mine was the birthday party.

We lived in a small neighborhood. Next door to us lived two women and a boy. The women were in the Salvation Army and had the distinction of being the only people on the street that our dog chased. He greatly disliked uniforms. My father wore one too, and did not always treat the dog kindly.

If the dog was not chained, he would chase the two women all the way up the street to the busy intersection. We would try not to laugh watching the women in their Salvation Army suits speed up their pace to avoid the brindle boxer named Pudge.

One of the women had a son. One had a man, but I suppose that he, like all the others, was gone to war. Later, he returned. I remember him walking up the street, because the sight of a man was so rare during the wars. He had hair graying at the temples and he was kind to us, buying us ice cream from the cart that came around. He would peek kindly inside the tent I used to make for myself beneath the spruce tree. It was one of my many hideaways. I was a child who could thrive on silences and solitude, finding everything interesting to my observations: insects, leaves, snails, even the very beautiful tomato worms that were my first childhood memory. I squatted in the garden, unhappily following my mother's rules. Against my own will, I picked these lovely worms off the plants and dropped them into a coffee can of kerosene.

▲   ▲   ▲

THE WOMEN'S HOUSE had rhubarb and hollyhocks that grew up on their own each year untended. I would climb the fence to pick red hollyhocks and entertain myself for hours, making hollyhock dolls while chewing on a stalk of rhubarb. Like my mother, I was alone. Unlike my mother, I chose solitude and its richness, even as a child.

It was from the window of the two women's house that one night I looked in on my mother. They were having a birthday party for the boy. It was a pitiful party, and I knew this even at my young age of five or thereabouts. Out of all the neighborhood children invited, I was the only child who attended. Even at that age, I understood it was a painful thing for the boy and his mother to have no guests but one. On this street, he was, for whatever reason, an excluded child. I hadn't wanted to attend. It speaks well of my mother that she had compassion for the boy and made me go.

Uncomfortably, I sat at the chair by the window, perhaps trying to visit or be friendly with the boy. But I noticed what took place around me. Something was not right with the women. The candles were placed on the cake before it went in the stove to bake. I smelled the wax when they melted. This made an impression on me. That I, only a child, knew better. That adults were not always smart or competent, not always to be trusted.

Wishing I were not there, I sat, uncomfortable, at the table, at the window that looked out and down onto our house next door. I was able to see my mother sitting alone, watching the television that had so recently become her companion, her world. She was watching *The Dinah Shore Show*, and I could see her in the faint light. Even without doors, looking in, I felt for the first time the silence, the distance, the clear knowledge that in this world I was on my own. As if her isolation, her history, was deeper and harder than any language could ever penetrate. I looked through that window and could see that she was deeply hurt by something I'd never know. I felt then that there was no room in her private, quiet world for me.

▲   ▲   ▲

THAT IMAGE OF my mother in gray light was a scene that stayed in my mind forever. She was also the woman who to protect me would one day throw rocks at a girl who'd come to the yard to taunt me. In this way, I must have known she cared, I think now, and wanted to protect me, a child as sensitive and vulnerable as she was, a child who inherited her mother's world. But there was also something in her that I didn't inherit, something that was not soft but hard; when I saw kittens run over by a car and cried, she said that I needed to be tougher. Otherwise I'd never make it in this world.

▲   ▲   ▲

THE IMAGE OF my mother through the window seems so small a thing, yet is so significantly remembered. It was the beginning of a child's consciousness. Maybe in all our lives there are such moments when a child looks both outward and inward at the same moment. Aware of women who had something not right about them. Aware, too, of my mother's compassion, which looks so significant in restrospect, when I, as a five-year-old, I fought against going to the neighbor's party.

I still see my mother from a distance in time and space, as she was then, through the glass of two windows, not knowing she was watched by her own daughter. And even now the smell of burned wax brings back this memory, as does the sight of hollyhocks. Just as the scent of straw, warm milk, and cattle returns me to the dairy and its silent cats.

As a child I became like my mother, with my own inability to speak. And yet, ironically, I became a woman who uses words for a living, who has a need to create beauty, for remaking the world, a part of it, a corner, like a woven web just repaired with a new line of silk.

▲   ▲   ▲

ONE TELLING MARK of my mother's history is the scar of a large oval burn on her leg. It was caused by a hot iron that, as a girl, she wrapped in cloth and took to bed in order to warm her feet. She tried to hide the burn from her parents for fear that she would be blamed for her injury. But the sore became infected and she was forced to see a doctor. By then, the bandage of cotton was stuck to her leg. That she was hurt and that she would be blamed speaks volumes. In her family, injury and illness must have been a sign of human weakness. She both feared punishment and expected no comfort. This trickled down, was passed down to my sister and me.

Like my mother, I, too, became wordless as a child. At one school they thought I couldn't hear. At another they thought me retarded. As for my mother, the pain of having to speak was too great for me. I'd inherited it. I only wanted not to exist. I was in psychological trouble at an early age, and unlike my older daughter, whose violence went outward to others, mine fell inward, an implosion, a black hole like those in swamps where nitrogen disappears, or in the universe where matter is swallowed. As for my mother, attracting any attention, being looked at, was painful and discomfiting. I was a child emotionally vulnerable. By the time I was in sixth grade, I was disturbed, crying uncontrollably, being sent home from school in hysterics. One time I was picked up from the bathroom floor after throwing a compass at a girl making fun of me. I threw it so powerfully it stuck in a desk. Then, at home, I was hit for causing trouble. I still occasionally wet the bed. By the seventh grade I was a lost child.

In those days, mine was not an eloquent silence, one chosen, but a miserable one. I was absent from my own life.

My older sister's life was somehow apart from ours. She was popular and beautiful and managed to escape. Passing for older, she worked in a hotel bar at the age of fourteen. She took dance lessons. She wanted movement. Looking back, I hardly remember her presence in the house. "Free" was her operating word. It still is.

And so, for the first eight years until my brother was born, I alone was present with my mother, the focus of her years of hurt, the one who would inherit her chemistry, fear, and depression. I was the one she hit with hairbrushes and yardsticks. My mother still laughs about how many yardsticks she broke over my four-year-old "behind." It is hard humor, a trait of the family. I, too, thought it funny until much later. My sister maintains to this day that I deserved to be hit. But shadows are cast in all directions, and all manner of falling. I was young then, my granddaughter's age now, and I cherish her skin, her flesh, in all its Korean, Lakota, Anglo body, her perfect feet on the earth, and I would not allow anyone to harm her, and this I call love.

▲　　　▲　　　▲

MY SISTER ONCE said, "You were different than I was. You wanted something." I said, "Yes, I was the fortunate one."

Luckily, I was the one who felt, who wept uncontrollably, who acted out, and feared. The one whose parents, at her own insistence, took her one night to the state hospital and watched as her feet were chained together and she was handcuffed for what was simply depression. No one spoke about it for over thirty years until I said to my father one recent day, "It must have been awful to see them do that to your daughter."

"Yes, it was," is all he said.

But I was also the one who searched, with all the emotional strength I could gather, and received, help, words, strength.

My brother was born when I was eight. It wasn't long after I'd returned from the hospital, having had pneumonia. I'd been delirious with a fever so high it deformed some of my teeth. Someone insisted my exhausted, pregnant mother take me to the hospital. A few weeks later, I was home, and my mother went to give birth to my brother, the long-awaited boy who, from my mother's European tradition, would enter the annals of this family as the one who would carry the family name.

My brother. Finally, there was someone for me to love, who loved in return. I remember the day he came home from the hospital. Our class was outside for recess and my parents stopped at the school to show me this new life who would become part of mine. I doted on him, dressed him. Bathed him. Played with him.

He was the male son, the uncle, the brother, who in an unspoken family agreement might have been expected to remain with our mother, to care for her. In my mother's family there were many of these men. There was something in the upbringing. There was Edward and his mother, Idonia, my great-aunt. One first cousin who stayed with his mother. There were "the boys," as they were called, three uncles who lived their lives together. My mother's family, from farming days, greatly cherished their sons.

With my brother this seemed to end. No son living with his mother, but his caretaking abilities were most significant and obvious to me when I was injured in a fall from a horse and he appeared daily at the hospital. On my release, he spent nights near me. At five in the morning before he went to work, he brought coffee to my nest, or spiderweb, as I called the little corner space in which I was contained for some months, unable to move.

▲   ▲   ▲

MY MOTHER INHERITED a tragic lack of generosity, an inner poverty I didn't, for many years, understand. When my husband and I married, she gave me twenty dollars to elope so I wouldn't bother her with a wedding. With it I bought material and sewed and embroidered my own wedding dress. One I still have. My husband and I married at a justice of the peace, in the living room with a statue of Sancho Panza. Afterwards, we had a steak dinner with two friends. We laughed about the twenty dollars at the time, but years later when I dreamed of a wedding for my daughter, I realized how sad a thing that was. With my daughter, I pictured how she would wear her beaded deerskin dress. She would be carried by our horse, also dressed in beadwork, even with beaded reins, as if they'd been made just for that purpose. I'd present her to her husband; we'd walk together up the dirt road with our traditional Lakota and Chickasaw clothing and I would give her to a man who would not drink, who would be kind. Needless to say, she eloped at the age of eighteen, the traditional clothing left in the closet and trunk. She came in with her boyfriend one day, with new comic books and two remote-control toy cars, to tell us they had taken their vows. She, the once-silent child, didn't have to tell me, though, I took one look at her and knew it.

My mother had no memory of my birth, offered no stories about me as a child. While I, unlike my daughters, had a family, I, too, had no history, just a few photos, stories told about how many times I'd been hit, or fallen off the bed, stories that, in our family, in our world, sufficed for humor.

I still asked questions, even at the age of fifty, because I wanted, needed, a history, a story, if only one, about my childhood. I was, in some ways, as without history as my daughters were, and like my daughters I hoped to find some filament of attachment with my mother that was never there. She was too sensitive, too unable to talk. She was filled with an unspoken pain I would never know or understand.

Though with time my mother has changed, she then, like my older daughter, belonged to what was under the surface of a world, in the shadows, behind the closed emotional doors of the bodily house.

▲   ▲   ▲

NOW, FROM MY unremembered life I try to put together my mother's world from pieces, notes from teachers on a report card, photographs. I try to assemble it, to tell a story of a disturbed daughter and a mother who feared phone calls, walking past windows, and going out in public. A mother who believed that everyone would steal from her or would hurt her. Something had gone wrong in her past. It was unspoken, unacknowledged, except for once when my father said these saving words: "Your mother isn't stable enough to drive a car."

I was older, my father was sick, and I was driving two hours to pick up my mother to go to another city, to the hospital, then returning her, before driving another few hours home.

My father couldn't have known that these words were such a gift to me, that finally someone besides myself acknowledged that something in our lives was amiss. Until then, I believed no one noticed how deep the silences went. Acknowledged, there was no longer anything to resist, to understand, to seek, and my heart softened.

▲　　　▲　　　▲

MY MOTHER MAINTAINED to us all that she'd had a good life. Once, one of my cousins called from out of town and came to talk to me about our mothers. Her mother, too, was a woman hurt, unable to even look at other people. Like my mother, like me, unable for most of my life to look up at a person, to speak.

With the women in their family, I can only surmise what must have happened in their lives. I tell myself the worst of stories in order to understand. I remember hearing a few of the wounds, in addition to the burn, that she had suffered. There were things she'd told me before the longer silences set in, her brothers holding her down and spitting on her face, her story of squeezing baby chickens too tightly and killing them—that sign of love gone so needy as to become destructive.

But it seemed as if, by and large, my mother's family didn't stay very much in touch, unlike my father's family, which called and visited and gathered together. Still, like so many men in his generation, my father as a young man suffered from a lack of emotional courage and strength. These young men had a need for self-protection. They were strong and competent in other ways, building a room, repairing a broken pipe. But they would leave when things were difficult or painful in emotional terms. Like the time we visited my father's brother, and my father drove away while his brother was still talking, out sitting on the well under the starlight, telling us about the recent sorrows and injuries in his life. It was a night of meteor showers, stars falling. For my father, it was sadness, not unkindness, that made him leave. The sadness of a long-lived man watching his family dwindle down to only a few.

I recall the conversation that night, for it touched me to see my uncle, the man who had been a cowboy, a farrier, a strong and handsome figure, sitting and telling about how he'd fallen from his horse. He was unconscious. His arm became infected and he'd nearly lost it. As he spoke he looked at his arm and said, "Look, how old," as if he'd only then, for the first time, seen himself. As if time had been lost and he had only just then noticed it. He was grieving. He'd just lost his dog, through drowning, the dog that had saved him from an attack by a wild boar. My uncle, alone, in a cowboy's house with saddles and bridles and halters, with tools, a strong man looking at signs of age in his flesh, the arms looser. And me, like my father, with my own need for detachment, only in a smaller dose, wanting to photograph his house, put a camera in front of myself, to keep for myself some of the world of our many men, uncles, cousins, thinking I ought to write a book about the Indian cowboys in my family, men young and old, who'd posed in the photographs dressed in chaps, with pistols, large Stetson hats (the dirtier the better), and rodeos always in the background of their lives. My grandfather was a wild bronc rider. I had always been proud of these facts. My own girlhood uniform made my sister pretend she didn't know me, the cowboy boots, a fringed vest, and now and then a hat. This get-up greatly embarrassed her. Even when I wore a dress it was with cowboy boots. She was image-conscious and also insisted I try to hold in my stomach.

My grandfather, too, never spoke. My father tells a story about his father. As a boy, my father tried to get his father to talk by waiting at a gate for his father to speak, after moving the cattle, only to provoke anger and not a request to close the gate. Even now, it hurts to see my own father as a boy, wanting, as I did, love and connection. And yet there we were, in a world of silences. My father has a great capacity for love, and an energy of talk, once you get him going. At eighteen, when I first confronted my parents about what I felt to be their lack of love, my father got up from the table and, angry, went out the door, then returned and told us that everyone he'd loved had died in the war, and his eyes were moist and I loved once more his honesty and self-searching, his ability to grow.

▲ ▲ ▲

NOW SOMETIMES MY life seems so far away. An Indian writer, a teacher, a person unlike the family I came from. Because of this, it was made harder. I have compassion for the many ways I have been lost by an American education. And for the things within me that, even now, will never find words, as if words are false in some territories, and they are not enough in others.

Exposures

THERE IS A photograph of my mother walking quickly down a street in Denver. She walks beneath a clock. She is beautiful, well-dressed, seemingly confident, and in a bit of a hurry. Where is she going, I wonder. What time is on the clock and in how many years will she be unlike this, having, like other women, lost her young woman's hope for the future, the hurried movement, the tall posture?

The change in her from then until her forties was a distance immense and secret. As I look back at her from the other end of time, it seems appropriate that she walks beside a clock. She is the woman who had choices she couldn't make, who would become silent instead of speaking, who would be betrayed, and for a time become heartbreakingly unhappy.

Between then and now there were hailstorms, car accidents, loneliness, sorrow, and anger.

▲   ▲   ▲

BACK IN THAT first, doorless home, my sister and I slept with our troubled dreaming in the next room over from our mother. Our dreams and my bed-wetting were evidence that something was amiss. We both had nightmares. Later we speculated as to the reasons and considered that our problems were not only emotional but also chemical. We lived in a world where DDT was sprayed on us to keep flies away. I remember the odor. It was my favorite smell from childhood. DDT was sprayed freely on the table, or any other place insects ventured. Mercury was also considered harmless at the time. Merthiolate and Mercurochrome, it was painted on our throats to keep us from tonsilitis and strep infections. We played inside rusted cars by the nearby dump that was later revealed to be a chemical waste site. Later, both of us sick, we recounted the many exposures of our girlhoods.

But for me there was, in addition to physical illness, an emotional component. My dreams addressed the silence and the powerlessness I felt. In them, I tried to seek help. They were dreams of helplessness, of darkness, ghosts, of trying to scream and having no voice, of running with all my might and standing still. In my dreams were closed doors I beat with bleeding fists and no sound would be made, no door opened. They were dreams of a frightened, disturbed child. In them a struggle played itself out. By daylight I was depressed. At night, in places of darkness, I was fearful and desperately wounded, and I seemed permeable, as if in that first house there was no wall between me and others, me and history, me and earth, so that even as I grew, the pain of others would hurt me. And yet, whatever wounds also sometimes heals. This was the step toward compassion, empathy, my gift, my curse.

▲   ▲   ▲

AT THE TIME, there were so many loveless women alone with their children, carrying the dead weight of nuclear families, with no one to guard them or protect or teach. Their soldier-husbands were in other lands doing what they would never speak or tell about themselves. Once, in innocence after watching a war movie, I asked my father if he'd ever killed anyone, and he went into an unexpected rage.

As for my sister and me, at night in that first house of my memory, we didn't sleep well. What was hidden in our mother, I believe, came to us at night, walked over the floor heater in the hallway where I had burned my feet and into the doorless rooms. While our young minds wandered, her fears came to life in our sleep, as if we dreamed her painful dreams, her monsters and wars and violence, ghosts like those who threatened just outside the door. What was never spoken expressed itself in us. She was so unlike my mother now, the one who sang "Happy Birthday" into the phone's answering machine. But then, as with the birth mother of Marie and Jeanette, the unspoken, turbulent, inside world surfaced in the children.

▲   ▲   ▲

NOT ALL THINGS are excavated or repaired or found. The statue of Colossus, the stone giant that made God jealous, was struck to ruin, but the stones were used again for other buildings and creations, and this, I sometimes think is what we humans do with our histories; we transform them into something better, if we can, something beautiful, creations of the daily sort.

I slid by somehow, I grew beyond the confines of a small life into a world of many kinds of relationship. And I still think of those Salvation Army women and the evening I saw inside our home from theirs. Salvation, itself, is an interesting word. From salvage. That's what heals us, that we salvage for ourselves from the wreckage of the larger life around us, or even from the smaller one inside. It's what humans spend their lives on. It's not so much a choice as it is a destination.

▲   ▲   ▲

MY MOTHER HAD sayings for every occasion. It was her language. They stayed with me as I grew older. They have sometimes seemed wiser and truer than I would have guessed: A stitch in time saves nine. Don't count your chickens before they hatch. Don't carry all your eggs in one basket. Womanly sayings that, in a smaller sense, took in the breadth of our chores, and in a larger way determined the decisions we would make in life, how we would think about the world, encompassing all our future experiences, and these have, as trite as they now sound, been a decent map of words to follow in life. Haste makes waste. Wishes don't do dishes. Don't look a gift horse in the mouth. A penny saved is a penny earned. If the shoe fits, wear it.

FIRE

Hidden Fire

IN A CREE story, Wolverine, an animal known for its intelligence and cunning, tells the other animals to hide their inner fires by closing their eyes, so that the jealous humans will be unable to find and kill them. The humans, it seems, envy the animals their grace and power, their radiance and life. The animals have a grace we believe we humans lack.

The closing of the eyes may have saved the animals from the people, but it also meant that they could not see, so were they safe? Perhaps Wolverine tricked them. Perhaps he was hungry that day. I do not know the ending of this story. But I do know that for us, to open our eyes, to see with our inner fire and light, is what saves us. Even if it makes us vulnerable. Opening the eyes is the job of storytellers, witnesses, and the keepers of accounts. The stories we know and tell are reservoirs of light and fire that brighten and illuminate the darkness of human night, the unseen. They throw down a certain slant of light across the floor each morning, and they throw down, also, its shadow.

Because of this shadow, I never know if I should let our lives sit in silence, undisturbed, disappearing, or if I should shake them, search them, and speak them so they are not lost, our lives not passing without meaning, or without telling. Nor do I know which of the stories of the past are true, but there are photographs in my father's family that tell a story.

In those of my father's family are men clowning around with pistols, looking dangerous and careless, wild men in fur chaps, Stetson hats sometimes on their heads, spurs on their boots. They were reckless young men. In one photograph, my grandfather, the man I had only known in his poverty, looks dapper in a greatcoat, walking through the streets of Ardmore, Oklahoma, like a businessman, my uncle and father hurrying along at his side, all of them looking like they had a good handle on the world. My grandfather was the same man who, years later, would hitch a ride to the streets of Ardmore to drink with the other Indian men, to sleep there some nights on the street. As a child I feared him. As a woman I think I understand him and how he fell into that world and life.

Indian Territory

MY LOVED ONE told me that almost asleep one night, in that twilight state where we hover between sleep and waking, I said, "There are eight people in this bed." It's true. Many fates dwell inside a single human being. We sleep with all those whose blood or lives we share, inheriting their histories.

Like everyone, I fell into the fire of all those other lives—my mother's, my father's, my grandmother's, my husband's, even those of the children I adopted to love and raise. In this, I became the meeting place of forces not my own. I must have known that there is something about the commingling of lives and spirits in all their randomness that makes for a spark of life that, like fire, creates change.

▲   ▲   ▲

ONE YEAR MY father and I went back to our homeland in Oklahoma. We were together in search of our world, our histories. We wanted to visit with some of the Chickasaw elders. As individuals, and as tribal people, my father and I were searching for ourselves. The American Indian Movement had gathered strength, and we, in turn, were strengthened by it. My father's own transformation was great, as if he'd held inside himself generations of anger and hurt that now found expression. At the time, we both received *Akwesasne Notes*, a native newspaper in which we read about the occupation at Wounded Knee and the people who were there in the early 1970s surrounded by the United States military, the FBI, and the nontraditional members of the tribe who had the cooperation of the federal government on their behalf.

That we had not, as Indian people, given up was a force of our returning strength. We still held the spark of ourselves, our histories, our future. Up until then, for many of us, it was as if we were beneath something, in a darkness sometimes lacking hope. The poverty rate was high. Large numbers of native women had been forcibly "sterilized," especially in Oklahoma and South Dakota, and children were lost from communities. A nurse at the Indian Health Service hospital at Pine Ridge said that one year all the infant children were taken from their mothers.

At the time of the occupation I was myself just beginning a life, just waking up. I'd been married, been divorced, gone to adult education to learn better to read, and enrolled in school with the unfocused hope that I would one day be able to offer something to my own people.

▲   ▲   ▲

AND SO WE went, my father and I, on a journey to Oklahoma, the place of my interior. It was not my birthplace, but it was my home, the place of my heart, my inner world, the place where I lived before I was born. Oklahoma was the place that shaped me with its loving people, beauty, and heat. It was where, always, I encountered kindness.

When we arrived, I was struck, as always, by the silence and stillness of our homeland. I have always felt it; a physical line crossed where suddenly everything is changed, as if I'm an animal recognizing territory. The air is heavier than in other places, containing the sensuous stillness of land, the rich, heavy odor of nut trees, the heat and the way it rises from the fields nearby. There were fireflies, and the rich smell of red earth and leaf mold. It is an ancient place, with plant fossils along the ground, and mountains so old they are underground, covered by what came later, depression sand storms, washes of clay.

Along with many other tribal people, we were just beginning to rest in our pasts, to look toward them as something most significant. Only now was it safe to return to the interrupted journeys our ancestors began, to look history in the newly opened eye.

Before then, like the animals, whose eyes Wolverine closed, we could not see. Now we remembered. We came from the mound builders, the brilliant calculators of time who stretched their hands in reverence toward the new moon and who touched the trunks and leaves of trees, their old friends, with grief to say farewell when they were "removed" along the Trail of Tears to Oklahoma, some in wagons, some walking. My ancestors were followed by thieves and the military. They would later be charged by the United States $720,000 for their own removal from their homeland. The Chickasaws owed money for food and supplies that never arrived, to those who coldly forced us away. Unable to leave their pets, they traveled with cats and dogs and the famous Chickasaw ponies that were a special breed. These beloved horses were stolen by thieves who followed along as the people walked west, and, bred with others, became lost, or so they say, in the recorded history of horses.

As an adult, going back to school, I remember finding a reference by Faulkner. He commented on a Chickasaw woman, just before removal, looking like royalty, he thought, in her purple turban. Even though we were the tribe that had never lost a battle, by the end of the removal we seemed lost.

We are from the Colbert family, of mixed blood, some of us in history good people, but not all. My grandmother, and maybe my grandfather, was the descendant of tribal leader Winchester Colbert. She was born in 1883 and lived through times that were filled with injustice and horror, the 1890 Massacre at Wounded Knee; it had roots in the fear of a very young federal government agent assigned to watch over an ancient, intelligent people who, at the sharp edge of history, were despairing. They called him Young Man Afraid of His Indians. It was the time of deliberate policies of starvation, wars with the multiple losses of people, animals, and land. The buffalo bones were heaped up by then, mighty animals killed only to subtract life from the world, an act none of us ever comprehended, even yet. Grasslands were set on fire to drive Indian people from their lands, and by then the waters were already polluted by pathogens from Europeans and their animals, pigs, and cattle. The new diseases killed the majority of tribal nations, and those who survived were forced to fight or move away. By then, too, wagons had eroded enormous ruts into the land. And last, there was the banning of Indian religions, religions that had kept the world in balance with song, prayer, and reverence.

▲   ▲   ▲

THE STORIES OF suffering that befell other tribes were continent-wide and traveled into Oklahoma. The United States government planned to place all Indians inside this seemingly insignificant place they named "Indian Territory," and then build a wall around it.

It was a dangerous thing to be Indian. My grandparents witnessed what some called the end of our nations. They survived through treaty-breaking times, gunpowder times, and finally the whirling sands of a deforested Oklahoma where even their trees were stolen by white men looking to sell hardwood for gunstocks. My father tells about leaving for the day, taking the wagon into town, and returning to find their trees gone. It was a time when it seemed that even hope itself was killed. And so, hiding our light became a daily necessity. Survival depended on it.

▲   ▲   ▲

MY FATHER AND I, on our journey to Indian Territory, visited a man named Pud Bean. Like everyone else in the county, he was nicknamed by my grandfather. We sat on his porch in Mannsville, Oklahoma, and listened to him and the insects. He had recognized my father, and he talked to us about my great-grandfather. Although a recent article had said my great-grandfather Granville Walker Young was a Canadian métis, he was listed on the Chickasaw rolls as white. My father seemed to already know the story of his grandfather, but no one had ever stated it so forthrightly as this elderly man. Granville Walker Young was ambitious and dangerous. He was enrolled as a white intermarried Chickasaw citizen. As it turned out, he was a thief, or so they say, of Indian lands, and, according to some, a hirer of killers. Yet he has always been upheld by history as a good man, held up just enough to throw us into doubt. Perched on the edge, we can't say for sure which side he fell into, the good man written about in history books, or the man who had a cold streak. Or, as happens in so many histories and stories, as is frightening about our species, he might have been a combination of the two.

▲   ▲   ▲

AT THIS SAME time, my mother's grandfather wrote in his journal about killing buffalo and how he saw Indians and they seemed peaceful. When I think of these parallel worlds, it's with the realization that I contain blood of both victim and victimizer. But I also hold that there are forces deeper than blood. It is to these that I look, to the roots of tradition and their growth from ages-old human integrity and knowledge of the world.

▲   ▲   ▲

MY GRANDMOTHER AND her sisters were disowned by G.W., as he is still called. It is said that he had wanted them to marry white men, but they chose Chickasaws. My grandfather and his brother-in-law, an attorney, spent a great deal of time and most of their money contesting the will. G.W. had left all of his money to his son. A few years ago, G.W.'s grandson, a man I knew only from our family reunions, was killed, along with his wife, by their own child. He drove home in his truck one Sunday morning and met them as they returned from church. He shot them outside their home. And it was to everyone's grief, for they were good people with a rare kindness. But a son who also had inherited the blood of two sides.

Bloomfield Academy: Grandmother

LIKE THE LIVES of all the other Chickasaw girls, my grandmother's life was influenced, in part, by missionaries in Indian Territory. Their purpose was to Americanize the girls. She and her sisters went to the Bloomfield Academy, a Chickasaw girls' school. I once found her graduation exercises in *The Chronicles of Oklahoma*. She played a piano solo at commencement. Her sister recited "The Lotus-Eaters," by Tennyson. The Reverend Burris, an Indian orator, delivered the invocation in Chickasaw. It was a mixture of traditions and worlds. The girls were educated as if they were white, but leaving school on graduation, they returned to their Indian world. They ended up, like most other Chickasaws in that time, in rural poverty, without water, lights, plumbing. They lived at this burned place where I stood, where my grandmother once lived, looking out on the man-made pond where cattle drank. As a girl, I had fished here, and caught a turtle larger than the circle my arms could make.

▲   ▲   ▲

MY GRANDMOTHER HAD been the light of all our lives. She was a quiet, tender woman. I loved and was loved by her. I admired her and longed to become like her, wanting all my life to become a grandmother. It was my goal. Even as a young girl I thought ahead to my later years when I would cook for grandchildren, create stacks of toast and platters of eggs like the ones she had served up to all of us cousins, uncles, and aunts, in the mornings.

Like most of the Chickasaw women, she was an active churchgoer, practicing the outward shape of Christianity while retaining, I believe, the depth of Indian tradition, a reverence for life, a way of being in the world, a certain calm and clarity. Yet the double knot of America was tied about her and inescapable. She lived outside the confines of the white world within an older order, holding the fragments of an Indian way. She was the face of survival, the face of history and spirit in a place even women were forced to take up arms to protect themselves. At death, she made a statement of resistance, a rejection of the American ways. Her gravestone reads, as does my grandfather's, "Born and Died in Berwyn Indian Territory."

▲   ▲   ▲

ACCORDING TO MY father, his mother was never sick a day in her life. Her only visit to a hospital was when she was burned by hot grease which spilled onto her stomach and legs from a kettle on the stove. Now, with pain of my own, I sometimes think of her suffering, the burning of skin, the most painful of injuries, the tissue of flesh growing over, and I grieve her pain, all of it, the history and grief of the times.

My grandmother was the woman who spoke to turtles and they listened, the woman who wore aprons and cleaned fish. She was the woman with never-cut hair, and I loved to rise up early in the mornings and help her brush it. She was patient with all of us running around her legs and feet. She used lye and ash to turn corn into white, tender hominy, cooking pashofa, a Chickasaw dish, in a large black kettle on the woodstove she still used into the 1960s. There were Oklahoma nights full of my remembered fears, wet heavy air, and fireflies, the smell of pecan trees, a land with tarantulas and rattlesnakes, the numerous and silencing sounds of gunshots in the night. The lightning flashes that revealed my grandpa coming home, sometimes drunk. This must be a widely told experience or story, for more than one of my friends tells the same story about her grandfather. Including the part about how his horse stood by waiting for him to come around the next morning.

She was a woman, forced into English, who used snuff and healed her children with herbs, home remedies, and the sometimes help of a black Chickasaw freedwoman named Aunt Rachel, a root-worker who lived nearby and came from the slaves once held by upper-class Chickasaws before the Trail of Tears.

When I was young, in truth, I knew almost nothing of her except that she was loving and kind. Somehow that was always enough. It was nearly all I would need in my life.

▲   ▲   ▲

ON OUR TRIP to Indian Territory, my father and I stood near my grandmother's house, which was now burned down. We stood beneath the remembered tree and looked at the ruins. There were broken dishes I remembered, lying on the ground alongside other discarded, burned, or otherwise broken goods. An instant iced tea jar still contained brown crystals of tea. I picked up a chip from one of the dishes and put it in my pocket along with the plant fossils from the "tanque," our name for the man-made waterhole. I carried away mementos not only for the memory and connection, but as if these things would prove my life, my tribe, my worth.

This is the sometimes dilemma of the mixed-blood person. We come from people who lived in a time when dances, with their central fire, were outlawed, gatherings suspect, languages forbidden. But, however broken or burned to the ground they were, many of us have risen out of the forbidden ways. It is the same way a frog wakes up beneath mud, smells water, feels rain, and digs out of the safe depths toward life and daylight, its internal fire still burning, its heart moving. I am one of the children who lived inside my grandmother, and was carried, cell, gene, and spirit, within mourners along the Trail of Tears.

As my father and I stood there, I saw the world with my grandmother's eyes. "Oklahoma," as a word, means red earth, red people. It is a term of connection. I always feel a certain love coming from the land itself, and that day I did; my grandmother's world remembered us. My father and I listened to the deep sounds of bullfrogs behind us, and I recalled the still Oklahoma nights of fireflies and bullfrogs, locusts, cicadas, running through the darkness with my cousins.

I remembered then reading a story about a man who tried to warm himself in the light of fireflies, and he succeeded, I believe, because it was beauty that warmed him, not fire.

▲   ▲   ▲

AS WE STOOD at the old house, my father's face looked sad with memories. I looked at him a long time, seeing it all there. This world, for my father, was superimposed on his life, and on a better world. And it showed on his face. Beneath his cowboy hat, suddenly he was tired, almost gray. I had the good fortune to be young; I did not possess the memories that inhabited my father. While I was sad for what was lost, because it was so much, I also felt a calm happiness that here, even in a burned place, at least a part of my life was held and remained. I had this, if little else, I told myself. It was important to me, a child born for relationship, one that would spend her life addressing the past and how it had become the present blaze of life all around her, how it could move into the future. This place was my foundation, even burned, even ash. Yet I grew up from it, and came as if from mystery to honor, love, and care for, all the alive earth.

▲   ▲   ▲

LIKE MOST OTHER Chickasaws, we became landless. We lost nearly everything. The Ardmore airpark was now on our land. My father told me what the old land had looked like, and from within myself, standing there with him in the heat and the smell of black walnut trees, I could see it beneath the airport. I could, with my mind's world, my open eyes, see what had been beautiful. Creek. Pasture. Pond. Valley.

After the Depression and dust bowl, after frauds and con men living off other people's misfortunes, the changes in his world had been unbearable for my grandfather. He was the son of a white banker and a Chickasaw woman. He'd been a rancher. He went to school at Harley Institute, a Chickasaw Choctaw boarding school. He was intelligent at algebra and, years later, after my father brought him a battery-powered radio—for even in the sixties they had no electricity—he knew every baseball player, who they played for, and their averages. An odd thing, I thought, for a man who had been so hurt by his losses.

Impoverished, the young men in those photos with guns and chaps and Stetsons, my uncles and father, went into the CCC and traveled the country. They received a small payment and the government sent the rest of their checks home to their mother. My father worked on the manmade Lake Murray outside of Ardmore, Oklahoma. He went on to learn stonemasonry and then to the art of grafting trees, so that an apple tree would give birth to peaches, a peach tree would grow plums.

▲   ▲   ▲

BY THE TIME of this visit with my father to Oklahoma, I had adopted my two daughters. The older was ten, almost eleven, when we adopted her. The younger was five. They shared the same birth mother. Adoption, like fire, was a life-changing event. It was not as easy as being a grafted tree. My father had learned to create trees that bore two kinds of fruit and would heal two together into one, and this was what I believed adoption would be, old trees bound with newly grafted limbs, bearing blossoms and fruits. With humans, it isn't as easy as trees.

After they moved in, and their story unfolded, I thought it was more than Wolverine who'd stolen my daughters' fire. Sometimes a person closes their eyes to keep fire in, unstolen. But it doesn't always work. The girls, too, had interior worlds inherited from others, a history dwelling inside them. Sometimes the thieves of fire are the closest people to you. You live in their house. It is by proximity, after all, that fire burns. And pain, in all its incarnations, physical, emotional, historical, is, like fire, a thief who changes lives and people irrevocably, a verb disguised as a noun.

With my own mother, she and I come from vastly different times and cultures. While we were related by blood, my heart came from some other place, from a tie to this continent. In her time as a younger mother, she mended underwear and darned socks, ironed and kept the house tidy. She had a mother's duties. She was disappointed in the adoption of my daughters. While I considered it a gain, a hoped-for tripling of love, she thought of it as the loss of a bloodline. I saw it as the strengthening of tribes, the future of our Indian children, back in their right place, open-eyed and knowing who they are. But the people of my mother's generation think differently from ours.

I was a proud mother, but she wanted our "own," the word that stands for possession, the small word with big meanings that had already damaged my daughters. Over time, though, worlds and people change. She has grown now, in all these

years, beyond those words into a kind of love, and a joy in her
great-grandchildren.

▲   ▲   ▲

I ONCE BELIEVED that love was a steady glow that would
light the house of life. The hearts of children would open. So
would the hearts of parents. I had room for love, so much to
give as if it is an *eternal* fire, like the ones my ancestors carried
over the Trail Where People Cried. And always, when confronted with smallness what I wanted to have count was my
own capacity to love. Like my father, I had survived history,
survived even myself. All of it. History. Mental hospitals. Alcohol. An American education. I look back now on the history of
a life; mine was one of a drunken young woman who once
went so far as to drink a bottle of peroxide and a bottle of
cough syrup together. Now it seems that young woman is
gone, transformed, as by the fire of life.

One day, not long ago, at my parents' house, as I cleaned my
granddaughter's face, my mother looked at me and said, "You
love them all, don't you?"

And I said, "Yes, every last life." Every last thing. Every creature.

▲   ▲   ▲

AS TIME HAS passed, things in me have been burned away
and I see my life more clearly, more cleanly, than I had ever
seen it before. And in that vision of my past, my history, my
body, I also saw there was something inside me that had survived and not merely survived but had done so whole and
nearly intact. The hurt child raises itself and doesn't just walk

but swims and flies. This child sees that life may never be easy but may be beautiful, as the story of the man who warmed himself by the beauty of the fireflies.

Fire, like pain, like love, is a power we do not know. Yet from the ashes of each, something will grow. No one knows if it will be something beautiful and strong. But in our lives, it is sometimes the broken vessel, as writer Andre Dubus calls it, that spills light.

DREAMS AND VISIONS: THE GIVEN-OFF LIGHT

Blue

I FIRST WENT to the glacier because a woman told me that there, in the ice, she'd seen God. It was a cold and foggy summer. I was on my way to Juneau by ferry and decided that, once there, I would visit her God and see if I agreed.

And so one morning I went to the top of the slow-moving glacier. We landed in the place by helicopter and were dressed in heavy clothing, which seemed inappropriate for a meeting with God. I couldn't decide if it was the power of mass, cold, or light that had swayed her so, but whichever it was, I agreed with her; peering down into the blue depths of ice, I saw the face of a god, one both beautiful and severe.

The name "ice" is not large enough for this brief sight into everything that is more powerful than human. Most striking for me was the brilliant blue light the ice reflected. It would be called otherworldly except for the fact that it comes from here. It was the light that dropped me into its world, pulled me toward crevasses and openings unsafe but divine. Standing there, looking in, I knew a fall would mean not only death, but being lost forever, entombed inside the break of light and ice. I had to say I wouldn't mind; against such greatness, I was too small to matter.

The blue light emanating from the deep cracks and openings in the glacier is light that can't be taken in by ice and so it is turned away. That is its science. And what's turned away is beautiful in its retreat. That is its art.

It is at the edge of ice where light changes direction. But boundaries and points of contact apply to other things as well. Dreams, I think, are like a glacier; they have light and resonance, science and art, and are in constant movement. Psychologist Marion Woodman calls them the "ancient portion" of the mind. Like glacier light, they live, also, at edges. Their borders exist between the human being and other worlds. They are the given-off light of our own human mystery, comedy, and catastrophe. They are what is too beautiful or frightening or powerful to be taken in. And, as with the glacier, a person could fall into one of them and be lost.

So how then has it happened that we've come to a world where we say, It is only a dream? Who would ever say of a glacier it is only ice, only light sent back to the sun, only one of the world's creations?

▲   ▲   ▲

DREAMS ARE THE creative store that is true wealth. They reside at the human edge of the holy. From the unknown, from eternity, into the restless minds of sleepers, their light is given off. In the human body, worlds are charted, wounds healed, illnesses reversed. In our vulnerable sleep, those hours when anything could happen. Like dark matter in the universe, dreams have mass and presence, even when not remembered.

▲   ▲   ▲

IN MY LIFE, I was always a dreamer. Every night I explored the understory of my life as revealed in sleep. Keeping a notebook by the bed, I wrote dreams down as if they were precious gems I could know or keep, dreams of water, of forests and birds. But there were two significant events in my life as an adult that, like glacial ice, were shaping forces. Both events, in their own ways, were about the loss of dreams. With my oldest adopted daughter, it was a dream of love, hope, and family that was lost by something already wronged, already beyond my knowing, a history that had injured her before my knowledge. And shortly after this first loss, perhaps even held inside its sphere of grief, was the second, an illness called fibromyalgia, that took away not only my bodily strength and muscular power, but also, because it is an illness accompanied by a sleep disorder, my ability to dream. For me, this was to be shaken below bedrock, to the fault line everything in the body is built upon, the vulnerable place everyone tries to pretend is not within.

Because I was always a great dreamer, the loss of dreams from the sleep disorder was a sign that something was amiss in the continent of my body. I'd had faith in my dreams. Now I no longer woke in the night to record the given-off magic of stories and places my mind would tell when my daytime vigilance relaxed. There were no more images that welled up from the world of night, from the body, the way water surges up to the ground surface of earth. There were no richly figured creations of something unknown to waking life, no infinite pathways unavailable by day. Their powers were now gone, and I missed a part of the inner imagination and beauty I had valued, the "ancient portion" of my mind. For me dreams had been the measure not only of the mind, but of the human spirit and connection with the world. My recurring dreams of wise old people who dusted pollen on my body now were gone.

As if losing the ancient measure of myself wasn't enough, the loss of memory accompanied my illness, and so did pain. Without sleep and dreams, there was, also, no night mending of the human body. The healing that used to take place in my sleeping body no longer occurred. While I might have been intelligent enough to find a way to live with external tyranny, no one is canny enough to handle an internal war; it is one that by its own nature has no winner, as if I'd turned on myself, and medically speaking, I did. The inner story slipped away from me, my self was dismantled, unbuilt. Each night I was falling from foundations I once thought secured, vaulted even. No longer did I give off light. My faith in the body and its vitality was lost, and losing faith in the body a person inhabits and has been in good relationship with is frightening. Being ill and in pain, no longer could I take for granted that I would be able to climb a flight of stairs, or even, at times, lift a glass of water to my lips or button my own clothing without resting afterwards, crying over what I had become.

It was as though I was being unmade, as Elaine Scarry says in her book *The Body in Pain*. In pain there is the unmaking of a person, an identity, a world. One becomes only, merely, an ache, a broken person. Perhaps the loss of self and identity is always a feature of disease and suffering. Interestingly, in many cases of chronic fatigue syndrome, one of the symptoms of this unmaking is that fingerprints, the mark of an individual's identity, disappear.

While not giving off light, the body yet has its resonance, its dark light of destruction, its aftershocks; when it's all pared down to its tragic core of survival there is often little or nothing left over. The faces of the ill are visible to me; the nearly paralyzed facial muscles, the inward-turned eyes of pain's depth, the inabilitiy to make the face muscles move into a smile. When I see other people on the street who suffer, I recognize them. It is as if the face is a map of the body.

Awaiting

WITH ILLNESS A person loses time, measured in days, months, even years. For me, there were lost years. There was the first year when I could barely get out of bed and was sometimes too tired, too aching, to dress. All of my money and time went toward the search for healing. Medical doctors, mineral springs, chiropractors, spirit doctors, acupuncturists, herbalists, and rheumatologists. I visited them all. I even saw a woman who sang songs into my body. Then I'd begin again, at the beginning of the list. Time, I thought, would heal me, even if the healing was death.

So for years, I waited. I hoped for healing. It was as if a tide had gone out, leaving behind a tide pool with stranded orange starfish, ghost crabs, anemones, and mussels attached to rocks, closing themselves, awaiting the return of water. In time, if the water didn't return, the pool would dry up. Like the stranded, I could only wait and hope, but in all that time, the sea with all its force and power had gone out and not returned.

The physical healing never came. Finally there were medicines that helped, but I did not ever return to what I had been before illness, nor have I ever been out of pain in all this time. That well-being of the past is now only a memory. I do not want to grace the state of illness because it is not a place of nobility. Yet, in some ways, I am grateful to have seen this underworld, to have been a stranded creature without water. For out of unwholeness something began to grow, generate. There were layers and depths of consciousness still not compromised. Like black rock formed by volcano, magma, or the black flowers philosopher Gaston Bachelard mentions in one of his books: "In the depths of matter there grows an obscure vegetation, black flowers bloom." For me, I developed, out of necessity, an empathy and a kind of spiritual growth. I was forced to live beyond my own body. This necessity seemed to have a given-off light of its own. Darkness, too, I know now, has its resonance.

The Unseen

WE HUMANS HAVE a belief in what is hidden and usually invisible to the naked eye; atoms, germs, God. And we call it the naked eye for a reason. In the history of the human mind, some have named this unseen, unknown part of a human the unconscious or the primal. It implies another mind at work inside us. It is the one that reveals itself in dreams.

According to turn-of-the-century psychoanalytic theorist Sigmund Freud, all we know and see of ourselves is only a small, pale tip of an iceberg. The rest is hidden, almost unknowable to us, barely reachable. It emerges without our knowing it, in accidents, urges, symptoms of hysteria, a word said that wasn't meant to be said. It emerges especially in dreams. These, Freud maintained, are part of the iceberg's expression.

In reality, Freud knew little about icebergs or glaciers. I suppose he'd never seen a real one and the way it gives off light, or his theories might have changed. While it's true there is a great deal that goes on beneath the surface, the tip is the part that is truly out of its element. It is the tip of the iceberg where blue light shines.

Freud's theories, however significant they may have been in their time and place, do not apply to native societies, dreamers, or visionaries who live in a larger version of the world. There are those with languages and spiritual leanings far more complex than Freud's theories of the culture-bound and insular, focused as they were on the individual. He took too little into account.

Carl Jung, a step farther, thought dreams were wiser than that. They had the ability to connect us with things not ourselves, but with parts of a larger world. His theories were more in keeping with tribal thought. But the unseen is more voluminous and beyond his imagining than Jung, too, realized. It often encompasses the psyche of a people, a culture. As with the visionary Black Elk's dream of horses, which resulted in a dance taken up by a tribe of people, and named the Horse Dance.

In this time of narcissism, there are those who believe that dreams are about the individual. The characters are ourselves, each component a part of the dreamer. If everything comes from one person's perception, the individual has far too much power and importance. This kind of notion is one not given to the idea of love, relationship, and ecology. It's as if the whole world, seen by and from one person, is merely a room with personal history and not that the person is a cell in the embodied world of spirit and matter. Dreaming does not carry this limited, singular, mission in all cultures.

Dreaming articulates the terrain of night, the range of a human soul, the geography of the holy, and draws a path to the divine. It is a map of sorts, one unknown to us by day. Dreaming is the point at which we begin to know. We are the dreamed, as well as the dreamers.

When writer Katherine McNamara interviewed Alaska native philosopher and writer Peter Kalifornski, he said that it isn't so much that people travel in dreams, but that the world speaks to people in dreams. What Kalifornski meant, I think, is that the sleeper is connected with the world. We are not solitary in our dreams. The human meets with the rest of nature, plant, animal, and the spirit world. This is why the location of the prey is dreamed by dwellers in the far north. As our elders say when in that state of meeting, that presence, "Something is there, something is about."

The Dark

WHAT IS IN darkness beneath earth has value. We wish to visit or learn it even while we search for what is far away; planets, galaxies, places, and events. It is not only the depth of dreams we search but beneath land, beneath water. Under earth, in caves and dark pockets.

It is in darkness that the sacred takes place, as crystals, stalactites, stalagmites, form in caves. Where opals grow their inner fire. What is rare and precious grows in dream light, darkness, earth, the cavern of sleep.

In the world of matter what is valuable lives, in much the same way, as in dreams, beneath the ground, just outside of human sight, sometimes just a bit beyond reach.

▲   ▲   ▲

DREAMS, WHEN SPOKEN, sometimes lose their power. And waking sometimes disappears them. Perhaps the uncharted mind wants to remain so. It is mystery we have always searched for, whether with the inner dimensions of a single person or in voyages across the world. Humans are always digging for the past with theories, beliefs, tools, and all the other fruitless efforts into unknown worlds. But I remember looking into the crevasse of ice, feeling small, knowing that we are temporary explorers who, after all this time, still know almost nothing about our world.

Dark Matter

CAPTAIN JAMES COOK, who had been sent to observe the transit of Venus in what was believed to be the tropics, ended up circling the south pole, amid islands of ice. The icebergs, blue in resonance, were enormous. Many were a hundred miles across and more, their light eerie, changing a people's sense of the world. The ice floes he thought "hardly worth finding." Yet, always, he and others searched. Because, it seemed, "the dream persisted, of the marvelous continent just outside the explorers' reach." Before Captain Cook searched the region of the Antarctic, it was thought to be a tropical climate. The journeys of James Cook, one could say, were also maps of dreams. He stood for a desperate Europe, this man, an ambitious explorer who wanted to be the first to enter the unknown wonders of the world. He circumnavigated the world, often lost. He and his men relied on the benevolence of the Native people who made great offerings and gifts to them.

Cook arrived, lived, and died by water and dreams. He found depth upon depth of ice mountains and polar, frozen ocean, places now being invaded in search for oil, diamonds, and coal, all shining things that come from the dreaming earth, black and glittering.

And now, too, we search the newly seen "dark matter" of space, and it is not, as was thought, empty. There is a density of what we now call "dark matter," and also journeys to the deepest parts of the ocean, to learn the creatures that have been hidden in the deep water of earth. We humans can never, even now, leave the unknown to remain with itself. Light emanating from a crack in the seafloor is thought to be bioluminescence given off from shrimp.

Other places are wholly dark; not long ago I watched on television as two researchers in a deep-sea vehicle, in the darkness, were searching this deep mystery, the depths of the ocean. An octopus hit their light. The men jumped back a bit, then laughed uneasily, wondering why it seemed to attack, even though it seems so obvious, that light was the intruder into the world of darkness. It seems certain that some darkness wants to, needs to, keep unto itself. Earth and ocean want their mysteries. It is not meant for light and human knowledge to shine into every unlit corner of the ocean, the earth and the universe.

The same men came across a squidlike creature with an eye

the color of blue sky, of water, of the godly blue glacier light. It was a large eye, one that could see much and measure what is seen. And so they captured the creature to take it to the light of the surface world, examine it, cut it, to its death. The squidlike being looked at them, its eye blue as sky, looking at the human who is frightened of unknown worlds. Like the glacier, the creature gave back what couldn't be taken in, horror perhaps of the men and their searching light, and then it closed its blue eye, as if it never wanted to see again. It was taken out of the depths and into light hard and cold, watched. One of the dreams, one of the creations of earth, was taken by men who are not of the dreaming, but of other passions, science and ambition and knowledge, a knowledge that has yet to keep the world alive, a knowledge at times of unbalanced proportion. The blue-eyed creature saw its fate. As did our Native ancestors.

Dreams and Divination

IN THE SOUTHWEST, the Apaches of Geronimo's band were known for their exceptional ability to outsmart both the United States and the Mexican armies. The United States and Mexican governments wanted Apache land for the copper and, possibly, gold and other elements that grew in the darkness beneath. They pursued Geronimo's band relentlessly. But the Apaches had a mysterious manner of vanishing completely when the soldiers and scouts thought they had just caught up with them and were about to attack their camp.

The success of this band of Apaches in eluding the governments' armies resides with Geronimo's chief military strategist, a woman named Lozen. Their success lay in this one woman's dreaming and her abilities to divine. Lozen was a political leader, a runner, and a good shot with a rifle. She was also a healer and dresser of wounds. Her brother Victorio, an Apache chief, said, "Lozen is my right hand." She was also, admirably, a raider of enemy camps, a horse thief, a healer, and a fighter.

Lozen, the warrior and healer, was a sacred woman, greatly respected by many tribes in the region. She was considered to be a holy woman and the guiding force of her people.

She was described by many as a beautiful and shimmering presence, light, holy. Her bravery was legend. Most important, she was something of a waking dreamer. The other men and women respected her greatly for her abilities to divine and dream. She was especially talented at locating the enemy. She became known as "a shield for her people." "I saw her many times find the enemy. She stood and sang a prayer: Upon this earth on which we live, Ussen (God) has Power. This Power is mine for locating the Enemy," she is reputed to have said. "I search for that Enemy which only Ussen can show me."

Once, stranded and hiding in the red dust of desert, she cared for a woman in childbirth. In order that they could escape from invading armies, Lozen swam a river upstream, against the current, to steal a horse from the Mexican army camped on the other side. She then returned and rescued the mother and child.

She was a warrior who rode alongside the men, as many women did, into combat. Once, at a dangerous intersection, where they had to cross the flooding Rio Grand with its dangerous currents, Lozen was described by James Kaywaykla, a young Cheyenne in the free band of Apaches: "There was a commotion and the long line parted to let a rider through. I saw a magnificent woman on a beautiful black horse—Lozen, the sister of Victorio. There was a glitter as her right foot lifted and struck the shoulder of her horse. He reared, then plunged into the torrent. She turned his head upstream, and he began swimming. The others followed."

There were, and are, many diviners in all tribes, but what made her invaluable was her "Power." The people believed that she alone among the band had the capacity to locate the enemy. To do so, she would stand with her arms outstretched and turn slowly in a circle as she chanted a prayer to Ussen. Her hands began to tingle when she felt the presence of the enemy. She could even divine how far away they were. James Kaywaykla, who later underwent decades of what he and others called a "skeptical education" in white society, nevertheless swore that he had seen her locate the troops time after time in this manner. Even after his supposed assimilation—if such a thing exists—he maintained she had such gifts and said that because of her abilities her people lived and remained for a good time away from their enemies. When she wasn't with them was when they met with disaster, and she was with Geronimo on his last uprising and was imprisoned with other leaders at Fort Marion, Florida, where she died.

▲　　　▲　　　▲

LOZEN "HAD THE power" of given-off light. She was more than awake. She was what, given another history, any of us could have been.

We Indians have always had great leaders who dreamed. Dreams are part of the spiritual condition as well as the intellect.

The dream world is a geography of sorts. Anthropologist Hugh Brody wrote a book, *Maps and Dreams*, about how the people of the north find their prey by dreaming its presence. The fact that many follow maps of dreams is an important testimony to its capacities. If it hadn't worked, it would not have been attended to; native people, by necessity, are practical people.

▲   ▲   ▲

THERE IS GRIEF I have felt in the decades since my own loss of dreams. I think of Lozen often, with water shining all around her, entering the river, saving her people for yet a little longer. I am not like Lozen, able to divine. I am ordinary and broken, but I know that we, as Native people, are awake and have survived. We have become something.

Perhaps dreams and a good heart are the antidote to a poisonous history. That day on the glacier, as an alive creature, the ice traveled. As it moved, the ice at the edge broke and crashed into water that accepted it into its own deep blue light. In its motion, it spoke in a voice which was the slow grinding centuries of movement and change. I heard it, and saw its light.

Seeing the new order of the old world is, in truth, a kind of light, powerful as that of a glacier and just as godly.

SPAN: OF TIME AND STONE

Friend, I will call a black stone friend.
— CRAZY HORSE

Breaking Stones

AS A CHILD, I hammered stones. I'd sit in a narrow alley or
a field for hours, breaking rock apart, opening the hardest of
objects to see what was inside. I knew there were secrets in
rock.

Older, I collected them, a piece of meteorite, a chipped
flint, the 300-million-year-old fish scale my daughter gave me,
a stone hammer with a place worn around it where someone
in the long ago had tied it to a stick or limb with sinew. Those
are the treasures. But as a girl, to hammer stones, it took faith
and hope, I realize now, a gambler's faith, thinking each rock
would be beautiful, would be a thunder egg or contain even so
much as a flake of mica. Yet it was always enough to find pink

granite or the common dark marl of any other color. Never did I find a rock that was ordinary.

What does it mean when a girl searches for secrets in rock? Maybe that she will become a woman who tells what's inside, that she will open hardness, that the interior will always be one of her searches. I still love the smell of stone, especially stone wet with warm rain and the tender promises of earth.

Mr. Frank

NOT SO MANY years later, at fifteen, I worked in a nursing home. There I first learned that the human body might, in many ways, turn to stone. Not only in the way it creates kidney stones or calcium deposits, but that some illnesses take away the joy of movement.

I was fifteen, and had just returned from Germany. I worked full-time as a nurse's aide in a nursing home. Mr. Frank, a patient there, had a severe rheumatic disease called ankylosing spondylitis. He lived on a high bed in a room without a window. The darkness of his room was powerful and heavy. It smelled of his breath, nearly all that was left of him. The table beside him was stacked with newspapers that we read to him when we had a spare moment from our duties of cleaning and feeding or turning patients, emptying bedpans, changing diapers. In this world of the bedfast, dying, and forgotten, it was his disease that frightened me the most. His tightness and rigidity made him seem angry. But it was more than that; it was terrible to know what could happen to a human body, that it might turn to stone. To get him out of bed, we would move aside the always unwrinkled linens, turn his feet and legs toward the center of the room, move him sidewise on his tall bed, then push down his shins and feet. Like a plank of wood, his body would rise to standing position.

He could speak only out of one side of his mouth, a mouth that could no longer open. He ate through a bent straw. He was unable to turn his neck. Sometimes he'd say flirtatious things to us. And now I know we should have flirted back, for he was not so very old, we should have given him a bit of joy.

Even though I was a girl who had already seen and bathed the dead, I was too young to think of how terrible it must be to be imprisoned, unmoving, inside bodily rock, to have no movement, to be a living statue. This man who could not bend, not even able to turn his head, scared me. Later, working in dental offices, I pored over medical books, always interested in what took place in the body. Pathologies of all kinds interested me, enormous goiters, children who had symptoms of old age by the time they were four. I was interested in medical conditions and how they came about. Too much of a chemical. Too little of a mineral.

For a time, I forgot Mr. Frank, because even if the older mind lives by remembering, the young mind survives by forgetting. I thought of him only years later when my own body began to harden. The body I had taken pride in because of the firmness of muscles and athletic strength, the flexibility that had so impressed my cousins that they still remember my abilities to touch my feet to the back of my head, do splits, and lift a leg straight up, my hand on my ankle. After I began to work and could afford it I took up skating. Soon I had a skater's body with muscular legs, because I skated each morning, renting what is called a "patch" of ice before going to my daily job in a Colorado Springs dental office. From my little area on the ice I watched Peggy Fleming skate her near-perfect 8's. I was not a competitor, just a lover of the grace of movement. I skated every night as well. And as I developed X-rays in the dental office darkroom, I stretched and moved, always physical, always an athlete. Even though there were years of my life when I drank heavily, I still made the glide across ice, smooth and easy, powerful at times. Or I would go dancing in town at night, driving by the clock near the Catholic school. Printed around the clock were the words "Love Makes Time Fly, Time Makes Love Fly." Wisdom wasted on people my age.

Temporary Being

TIME IS A familiar stranger. We travel through it, deceived and tricked by it. The prophet Isaiah promised the king that he could cure him by reversing the flow of time, light, and shadow. The Spanish searched a continent for the fountain of youth. Still, immortality is continually pursued by searchers, doctors, and scientists.

The desire, against time, has sent science into the secrets of cells and genetic materials in an attempt for modern medicine to halt or reverse its constant flow. Once again, for kings, not paupers. We are not so far away in history and time from those early European men traveling oceans to this continent searching for immortality and riches.

Galileo tried to measure time by his own pulse, and it was told by light and shadows, their lengthening, their descent, by passages, vistas and seasons, and even by animal migrations. Then, time was also measured by how quickly a stick of incense burned or by sand falling through an hourglass.

Now we have nothing so large and magnificent as all of these, only the ticking away of our days, our lives lost in it. As the Maya said, the day went walking, and as it goes, it takes us with it.

We are fortunate but temporary beings.

Gods and Other Carnal Matters

HUMAN MYTHOLOGY, EVEN with its many immortal gods, is about carnal matters. What are stories if not the containers of culture, the body, and its inner worlds. Myth encompasses many elements; the human and divine, the history of a people, their thought, their way of being, the terrain in which they live. The Greek god Kronos was one of the gods that represented time and earth. The father of Zeus, he was kept prisoner by his son on an island at the edge of summer sunset. His homeland was another continent, a place beyond what the people of the time had yet mapped. He was exiled to an island by which the sun could be measured in its seasonal change. The island was a set point for telling the time of year by its movement.

Kronos, like many other gods, represented not only time, but pain and aloneness. Perhaps that was why the word "chronic" derived from his name. It means something existing in time.

▲   ▲   ▲

THE GREEK AND other gods from around the world, with their flaws and fighting, suffered in the same ways humans suffer. I like them for this, their conditions of humanity. Not only were they time-locked, as we are, but they were amorous and jealous. I think of the jealous passion of the goddess Pele, in the Hawaiian creation story; the Pueblo first man who came up from the lake only to be wounded by the animals; the earth mother of the Mohawk who was pushed down to earth by her father. In some tribes, there were conflicts in other layers of the world that forced the humans into this one. Betrayal, physical pain, the whole frail human realm was held within the stories of these gods. They were not so different from us. The gods suffered, loved, and were sometimes healed. Their stories, like that of Kronos, originated from the natural world. The stories of gods and godlings not only explain us to ourselves, including our vulnerabilities, they go farther and explain the world to us, too.

Chimayo

ONE EVENING MY younger daughter, without explanation, had an urge to drive several hours to New Mexico. She packed her husband and children into the car and headed southwest, the children asleep, the husband humoring her. They drove through the night. In the darkness of their travel along a quiet highway, she suddenly told her husband, "Turn here." He turned the car to the right. Late at night, in the desert with its fine turn of stars overhead, she got out of the car and picked up some of the earth, not knowing where she was or why. She gathered up a container of earth and took it home with her.

"All I knew was I had to go there," she told me a few days later.

I was intrigued about her journey to this unfamiliar terrain.

We tried to ascertain just where they'd turned right. I showed her a map of the region, and together we found the location. She had traveled, without knowing it, to the famous place of the healing earth, near Chimayo. She had gone not to the sanctuary or church, as most do, but to the source itself, the place from which the earth is brought for pilgrims to touch and take home. She had gone to its place of origins. How did she, a Lakota, know about the place where she was compelled to go? I can only suppose the answer, that there are places that beckon, as iron to the magnet, a geology that calls us with its properties, a geography of healing. There are places deemed sacred sites by people who have known and inhabited the land for tens of thousands of years.

There are places of power on the earth. They have meaning not just because humans associate meaning with them, but because they resonate. They are designated sacred places not only because of stories humans tell about them, but because of the energies of the places themselves. They are alive. Stone. Clay. Mica. Minerals. They are associated with healing, or with other kinds of aid. They may be mountains, they may be a bend in a river, but they are sacred sites. Aetna, Mount Taylor, Mount Graham, Turtle Mountain, Ararat, where the ark was said to stop after the flood.

There are different stories about Chimayo and its sacred nature. In one, a holy child wanders the valley at night, healing sick children. This is the story taken up by the mission priests and their followers. But for earlier peoples it is "a place of good obsidian," a place where the ancient fires of creation left behind dust with medicinal powers, writes George Johnson in *Fire in the Mind*. For the native peoples in the region, this place my daughter divined has long been recognized as blessed earth which has "great medical powers that can cure pains, rheumatism, sadness, sore throat, paralysis, and is particularly useful during childbirth."

I've visited the sanctuary at Chimayo a few times. I visited with my family, alone as well, looking for healing earth. Once it was in early autumn. The earth smelled of clay. The cool, damp church smelled like the wet stones I recall from my childhood in the alley.

Inside, candles were burning. In the back room is the "Posada," the hole in the earth containing the soft red clay soil. Along the walls of the sanctuary are the testimonies of healings, discarded crutches, casts, wheelchairs, photos, and letters written by the healed.

The mineral world, it must be, makes its offerings to us.

Crazy Horse

"BLACK STONE. I call a black stone friend," sang Crazy Horse.

Before he died, Crazy Horse told his people, I will return to you as stone. There is no likeness of him. He was a beautiful man who loved his people. I try to imagine what he meant by those words. Perhaps he knew that a man's life crosses over into other elements and matter, but I can't know. I do know, however, that he said he was a relative to stone and wore a stone under his arm. It was given him by a medicine man named Chips. And I know, too, that the stone people are helpers for the Lakota as they are for other tribes. Now, western medicine uses calcium, lithium, boron, and other mineral medicines, as well.

My daughter, from the Crazy Horse band of Lakota, in her quest that night, was not so far off. She comes from a long line of Lakota women who know the properties of stone are powerful. They call stones "the oldest part of creation." They are women who doctor with stones. Every contact with a stone, the women say, is one of mystery and spirit.

MYSTERY

I LOOK OUT my window and see the wild horse. Mystery is her name, even her nature, but I usually call this Bureau of Land Management wild mustang Misty, for short. She stands in the red and gold of autumn leaves beside my older horse. She is sturdy, rock-solid. A wild horse, she is different from the other horses, who were bred for certain traits. Her eyes are set more broadly across, in order to see dangers and farther distances. Her lung capacity is stronger. She lives on less food than the other horses, and has hooves, as the Navajo say of their horses, made of agate.

Her black face is solid and it is haunting. She is so like earth that the large old trees standing nearby seem fragile. She matches the land. Blue roan in color, she changes according to the season. At times her coat is snow, at other times the color of sky, earth, or shadows. Last winter she had longer belly hair, the red of water willows as they change toward spring. Blending in is a desirable trait for an Indian horse. In the past, different kinds of horses were prized for their invisibility. Comanches and Apaches had great horsemanship and could ride unseen by a group of American soldiers by holding on and hanging their bodies on the other side of the horse, with only a hand visible.

For a long time out at the farm where I'd kept her, I watched Mystery stand and look at me with a slow, steady gaze, an occasional blink of the eyes. I tried to avoid her eyes. With them she seemed to claim me, but she belonged to another person, one who rarely came to visit. Occasionally I gave her carrots, placing them on the ground or in her feed so she did not think they came from my hand, so she wouldn't expect something from me.

Yet she began to grow on me. I had been trying not to love her, but failing. She was pregnant, and it wasn't long before I took out a folding chair, sat near the barn, and stayed around to watch the new foal move inside her, a turn, a light kick. Before long I knew, or felt, that she would, somehow, one day be living with me. So I began to brush her and feel her round, pregnant stomach.

I knew the owner hadn't paid the board on her, and I told the people who own the farm, Ted and Lori, that if her board was never paid, or if it happened that they would sell her, I'd pay it and buy her. The owners, as it happened, wanted her only for the foal, which they thought would be a black mustang. They called this Mystery ugly. But to me, she was most beautiful.

I don't know if Mystery was like the Chickasaw ponies I'd heard of in our own history, but she greatly resembles a drawing of one of the ponies. Maybe it was because of this that we had an affinity for one another. When we walked together it was at the same pace and rhythm, as if we were the same animal, not as Indians first thought when the Spanish arrived, men so afraid in the "new" world that they wore armor even in the heat of summer. Perhaps our affinity was knowing that she and I survived the same shared history. She is an Indian horse, if ever there was one, as Lori says.

Soon I began to walk Mystery down the road from the farm to fresher grass. One day a young buckskin from a neighboring range saw her, ran around the barn, and got another horse to come look at her. They stared at her with curiosity. Mystery, the horse branded U.S., with what looks like a bolt of lightning behind the letters, numbers frozen white. They were supposed to be identifying numbers, but they had faded away from America, the way so many of us have, horse and human.

That day, she lifted her head, gauged the buckskin, then went back to her work of eating the field. It reminded me of my Chickasaw father saying that when he was a boy, "Wild Indians came to the house, in loincloths and everything." He said it as if they were different from us. They were Apaches or Comanches, he thought, or others known for their great horse-manship. The men from other tribes came to be with our grandfather and my dad would go look at them. He and I both now wonder why they went to my grandfather's house. But that's how the buckskin looked at Mystery, the way my father, as a boy, once did with the men from other tribes.

Then, one day as I walked this pregnant mare, she got down on her knees.

I remembered reading that some of the Chickasaw ponies had such short necks that they ate this way. With Mystery, I thought it meant that she would soon give birth. That evening, I packed my car with clothes, flashlight, a miner's headlamp, and all I would need to spend a night waiting for her to give birth. It was going to be a wonderful night, I hoped, and I looked forward to seeing the new, beautiful life.

▲   ▲   ▲

EARLIER THAT DAY, Ted had made a manger, a shelter with fresh sweet-smelling straw. As night fell, Lori and I hid on straw in a dark corner waiting for Mystery to give birth. The plug came first. The vet stopped by early and confirmed this. He said it could be an hour or five days, shrugging. He's a casual guy, but I like that about him because it sets a person, and a horse, at ease.

It was late, so after a while we went into the house and had pea soup and bread and butter while we prepared for a long night, then Lori and I went back out, because I didn't want to miss the birth, but also I was worried about her, the four-year-old mare, who was young to be having a baby. Also, like the Chickasaw ponies she is small, only thirteen hands.

▲   ▲   ▲

WE SAT DOWN in the dark corner on fresh straw to wait. We were quiet because sometimes a nervous young mare will pull the infant back inside with her powerful muscles, and smother it.

Soon, we both sensed that something was wrong. Then a bubble began to emerge. Lori said, "I've been around horses all my life and I've never seen that before. I don't know what that is."

And then Mystery began thrashing, rolling around with pain. Her pain was so great that once she got up and tried to drown herself, shaking her head in water as a horse did a month ago, just before he died. And then she was down again. It was almost unbearable to watch such suffering. Her eyes darkened with the pain.

We tried then to get her to her feet so she wouldn't injure the unborn foal. Ted came out, and then we saw the foal's ear coming out first as if to listen to what kind of world it would enter. But in a normal birth, the front legs come out first as if the foal is swimming into the world.

The vet came back an hour later. We were all dodging Mystery's hooves. She'd turn over, hooves in the air, and we'd run from one side to the other, the arm of the vet inside her trying to get the foal moved into the right position, he having to be keen and alert in order to keep himself from being hurt, an arm broken, we running from side to side to avoid her hooves all the while we tried to get her to stand up.

Finally the thrashing and rolling had to end. The vet said the infant had already died of a broken neck. It could have been the thrashing, he said, but I wonder sometimes if he might have broken it in order to save the mustang. She would probably not have lived if the foal remained alive. It would have kicked an organ, an artery. It would be rare for a mare to survive this.

It was a long, hard effort to get her to her feet.

"Go get a whip, Linda," Lori said.

I looked at Lori, a full look in the eyes. I can't do it, I thought, I couldn't whip her.

Lori read my mind. "You have to or she'll die."

I picked up the whip and returned. I felt it would be impossible to hit the suffering horse others were already kicking and whipping in order to get her on her hooves into the trailer and to the hospital. So I stood in front of her and raised my arms with great strength, as if to show her. Somehow, magically, she knew what she had to do. She rose up and walked right into the horse trailer. I was thankful I did not have to hit her, thankful she was in the trailer. By then I loved her. I had compassion for her. And finally I knew that in spite of my soft heart, I would have whipped her if I had to, in order to save her life.

At the hospital, in a small pen, they shaved her and gave her an epidural, and her face leaned against the pen in front of me, exhausted, grateful to be free of pain. She exhaled. The other vet worked inside her. He said she'd had a broken pelvis, probably from when she was rounded up from her wild herd. At the roundups many are often hurt and killed.

Then I went around and looked at the foal; he was enormous and beautiful, wet and broken. And the shaved area at the end of Mystery's spine looked like the old hide paintings, as if there were patterns and stories on her skin, history written there. I would rub this place softly until after the hair grew back in and think of her story and how it was, in ways, the same as ours.

The next day, when she returned in the trailer, her eyes were crying. And after that, for some time, she would turn around as if looking for her baby and cry tears.

Mystery, for some time, expressed milk from her nipples to the earth. It broke my heart. And she would cry, looking around for her foal.

And now she stands, a beautiful survivor, as if she is sister to me in some kind of time from before. I look at her and wonder always if someone I came from knew her ancestors. Because with Mystery, it was not just her sturdiness or wildness, not the loss of a foal, that brought us together. We had these other things in common, a shared history, a world we once knew, the ache of being rounded up, being branded, owned, and battered.

▲   ▲   ▲

AS IF CONFORMING to her name, it was a life-changing accident and a world of shadows that led me to this small mustang. Along with this path, there was a strengthened return to my own world and tribe. Ironically, Mystery and I had an injury in common. We both had pelvic fractures, though hers was certainly more traumatic than mine. Her fracture began in the terrifying roundup of wild horses, mine in a fall from a horse.

Juncture: On Memory and Forgetting

OUR LITTLE TOWN is built on a hillside, a valley and two creeks. Four horses roam freely here. It is not unusual to come around a bend at night and find them standing together and unyielding, car lights ignored, beautiful and surprising only to the human. There are only two main roads. They meet at the top of a hill. A red horse once lived at the place where the two roads meet and become one. In that place my life fell against the world of the horse.

It was a warm autumn day that I went to that branching of roads, a day that began without shadows, in full light. It was late morning and a very fine day in my life. I woke up and phoned a friend before I went over to ride the horse I was hoping to buy, a roan Tennessee walker. "This horse," I told her, "is going to change my life."

I felt it already in my body, a growing closeness to earth, the grounding to a beautiful gravity that would later prove to be a closeness to death. There was a movement of life energy that I felt, a strengthening or quickening, and a solid peace. I watched two hawks in the sky, and the world smelled of dry leaves, horseflesh, and near winter.

"Big Red Horse" was what they'd been calling him, and I'd determined it was a name not good enough for him. I called him my new name for him, a word for the best of conditions within the world, a harmony, a concept not easily translated into English. I'd thought this horse would be a helper along my path to harmony, embodiment, and my own connection with earth.

On this sunny morning, who would have thought that I'd wake up three weeks later with almost no memory, or that at the age of fifty-two in a hospital room on a sunny November day, I would be crying, without even knowing it, into the laps of my parents and weeping against the wide shoulder of my brother? Or that months later I would be a different person, haunted by the memory of who I had been, thinking of *her* as another person on the other side of wounding.

For two days before that first ride, I fed and groomed the horse, taking him a few apples, and many carrots. He would lift his leg at a touch so that I could pick clean his hoof, and while I did, thinking he was so cooperative, I could smell the first hints of a winter whose magnitude of pain I would later forget. That day my thoughts were on the future, not the present, not the past. They were on the grooming, the building of the shelter, the manure cleaning, long rides along the trails and road where I live, and the pungent bark of trees. This was the time I'd waited for since my childhood in a family of cowboys.

We, the man who was helping sell the horse and I, had made a deal. The free board of his horse on my land in exchange for some labor and riding lessons. It seemed perfect. I was overjoyed at such an opportunity.

I was so overjoyed to have a horse, I didn't think clearly enough. I overlooked the smell of yesterday's alcohol on the man. I didn't ask neighbors about the horse and the horse-seller, new to our town and soon very unwanted by many neighbors in our small community. That day as I went over to ride Big Red Horse, I'd taken my helmet. The young man representing the horse-seller said he thought it might make the horse nervous, it might "freak him out," because it was such a gentle horse that it had never yet seen a rider in a helmet. Believing him, because he sounded so knowing about horses, I left my helmet by the fence.

The young man first placed his own Western saddle on Big Red Horse. With this first saddle we, the horse and I, rode up the hill quite beautifully and made an easy, gentle turn. Then, because the stirrups were too long, I returned and we tried a second saddle.

On the placement of this new saddle, nothing felt right. The horse stiffened, and I felt it, but I told myself the anxiety was my own, not the horse's. And also, if feel and instinct were a part of people's decision-making, the world would be so much finer than it is.

It was a cruel-looking saddle, black with squared, silvered edges. I thought the horse didn't like the person who used that saddle. Now that I know horses better, I can say that the saddle didn't fit the horse. And with such a strong feeling I would not, now, ride, because the bond between rider and horse is a connection, an agreement and negotiation that has to be mutual, and that day the red horse disagreed. The stirrups were still too long, so the young man made a quickly pulled-together correction that, later, either failed or caught my foot in them.

From the hospital weeks later, I had a fleeting recollection that the saddle was sliding sideways and I could only grab the mane. In a ray of memory coming through the darkness of that long forgetting, I know—almost—everything that had gone wrong, and everything the young man did was wrong. I was riding alone because his girlfriend, who boarded the horse, was angry at him and wouldn't let him use her horse to ride with me, a near beginner. She was angry, too, about the horse being sold, because the boarding fee was part of her livelihood and she didn't want to lose the two hundred dollars a month. Unknown to me, she'd already had an altercation with another neighbor who had offered free boarding to the owner.

So much is revealed in the aftershock of an accident, like how the horse had thrown three other people, how the young man one midnight was walking, staggering, drunk, on the highway trying to find the horse after it threw him. There were neighbors who complained about the treatment of the horse, said that the man rode it drunk late at night, up and down the steep and dangerous cable road in our town. But by the time it took for all the stories to be told, it was too late for me.

I will never know if I tried to jump off, if my foot was tangled in the stirrup or latigo, or if I was thrown. That forgetting is part of a head trauma, as if the amnesia protects a person from terror.

Partial Recall

THERE IS A strangeness to amnesia from a closed head injury. It consists of a floating mind, a sliding of time. Even now, much later, I lose memory. Asked about last Christmas, I find the events of the day disappeared from my mind.

Memory, I realize, is not a road from the mind, as most believe, so much as it is a path toward something, a source. It is a source that carries us into the future. "Some live in order to remember," writes Malidoma Some, "and some remember in order to live." For a time, I would be doing both, remembering and forgetting. Three weeks were gone from my life, the events of those weeks forever unrecorded by my injured brain.

On that day, with this floating memory, I remember, or think I do, there was a hole on the right side of the road. It was nearly invisible, covered over with dry, long, wind-bent grasses. I saw it clearly and suddenly, and I knew the horse would break his leg if he stepped in it. I pulled him to the left in order to avoid this. I remember, or think I do, that something came toward us; I thought at first it might be a dark motorcycle, a black bike, or a walker in dark clothes, coming toward the horse. All I could be sure of was that the horse flattened back his ears, turning in fear, and running. The problem with this memory is that the horse ran up the dirt road *toward* the moving shadow, not away as would have been natural if a horse, being a prey animal, was going to bolt from something on the road. At first, in the hospital, I said it was a motorcycle, but as snippets of memory come back, I can no longer say this is so.

In the dangerous first moments of the accident, time slowed down so I could see all that was wrong, but not until it was too late to correct even if I'd known how to change things. Every possible thing I could have done in order to slow the horse was the wrong thing. Even as I was forced to lean forward to grab his light red mane, I saw that he had once been injured there, and the very act of leaning forward, I know now, said to the horse, "Run faster." In that slowing down of time, I knew this touch would hurt or frighten the horse. Mine was the wrong language. The horse and I, at that moment, spoke different languages, and his was not conflict-free. As I was being helped onto the horse, the young man said his previous owner had called him Eros. So then, still in that stop of time, hoping he understood any piece of human language, I called the horse by his older name, Eros, that name just learned, and in that moment on the horse, I remembered that someone had told me that the previous owner had committed suicide. I wondered, later, if he had abused the horse, had possibly even tried to kill himself while riding, because this name frightened the horse even more. The communication between the horse and me was broken, or worse, never formed. And the horse, by his name, had been perceived as something less than horse, a human concept, a story.

My memory for human things was ruined. I wondered later why I hadn't grabbed the saddle horn, and recalled, vaguely, the saddle slipping toward the left. I had been ignorant and trusting and not paid enough attention to how the horse was saddled, not that I would have known then if it was right or not. I was a person who had faith and trust in others. This time my trust was wrongly placed, and joy became my downfall.

Later, I wondered if the something dark that came up the road was the young man who rented a room from the woman who boarded the horse. He rode the horse for free, and wanted to keep him. He had earlier tried to spook Big Red Horse when I was grooming him, clapping his hands in the face of the horse, passing them before Big Red's eyes. But it seemed unlikely that he'd be the one the horse ran toward.

These are only facts, not accusations, but it has entered my mind that maybe human smallness and two hundred dollars a month were what nearly killed me. But then, after the unre-membering of a changed brain, it could have been something as light as the wind that touched the red horse. Or a spirit from the invisible world. I will never know.

Forgetting

THREE WEEKS LATER I woke up and found myself in another ambulance as I was being transferred, the second time, from one hospital to another. And here, I thought I was awake. I thought I was steadfastly anchored in time once again, leaving the shadow world partly behind, still wondering what had happened, if I'd been in a car accident. Over and over again I asked what had happened to me. For over two years there was short-term memory loss as events failed to lay them-selves down in the brain. Even now, I forget last week, last month.

I only remember, from all the darkness, seeing his mane, his ears fully back, then darkness, and nothing, a lasting darkness. The distant sound of a siren. The urgency of the ambulance drivers, a one-second moment of fear that I was dying. I asked first, even at the hospital, if the horse was okay, more con-cerned about him than myself, afraid that whatever I saw com-

ing down the road might have injured him. I remember, faint-
ly, the sound of stitches being made in the back of my head.
The brief distressing sight of my blood, too much of it, on the
yellow cloth board on which they'd carried me, pools of it on
the floor, my daughter Jeanette tells me, she was so certain I
would die. The hospital called her and told her to come there
"immediately." She was slow and already grieving because her
foster grandmother had just died that same morning.

I woke up again six days later for a short while, and then
went back into the darkness of another dimension, unknown
to most, where life floated like something in water, toward me
and away in drifts and waves I didn't know until weeks later
when I woke up in that other ambulance on the way from the
head injury hospital to a rehabilitation hospital. Thinking
then that I was for the first time awake, I would nevertheless
later forget most of my stay there. It floated away into the shadow world with the other moments and days of my life. Later,
returning for physical therapy, I did not recall the people in my
daily life. Yet another part of me was awake. My journal was
full of those very people, as if a stranger had been writing,
using my hand. I wrote that I rode my wheelchair, looking at
the clean, perfect lines and limits and corridors of my world
now. Like veins in a body which is operative only in a certain
order, not human, not spontaneous, not breathing. I can't turn
where I want, I wrote.

I existed in a constantly forgotten presence. A word spoken
has no echo and disappears forever.

There is, as with riding, a fine art of walking, a quality of
remembering, and that of forgetting. Relearning to walk, I
tried to remember the softness of a foot touching earth but not

lingering, only touching, like a small prayer, skin on ground. Then there is the arm which must be made strong, straight. I worked hard just to move, to turn a chair, exhausted. All, finally, that was never there was a strand of a story, a hair from a horse's mane. This is how it returns, when it does, like rays of light passing briefly through a window, falling on the floor, momentarily bright. But there is a current of love passing through here and I am on it, learning the quality of walking, riding a horse, of being a human.

▲   ▲   ▲

I WAS IN another geography, the mixing zone where things meet, visions are revealed. It is a forgotten world, with unknown features of its interior. It is a place that has no language, no history.

Floating, Shadow World

IN ALL THIS time, I didn't realize the great falling away of light that had taken place in my life. In an injury like this, meaning escapes language and description. I don't remember that I'd try to say a word but another would come out, that I didn't recognize my daughter, that she had to feed me puréed food by spoon, that there was a possibility I was going to be permanently damaged.

I didn't even know that a brain was injured from a hard impact, hitting the ground hard enough to knock loose the bones in my ears. One of my lungs had collapsed from the fall, keeping even more oxygen from reaching the brain. I broke my pelvis in several places, and suffered a broken tailbone, elbow, ankle, sprained neck, and numerous other injuries. My daughter said my abraded skin looked like the skin of a giraffe.

In this state, a person is lost between worlds and selves. And at night or when tired, I began talking, as if another person were there. It was an entire conversation I couldn't stop. Now it was as if there were two of me. The one of the past, the one of the immediate now. The mind looks at itself and earlier memories of what it once knew or did. It remembers what it used to be.

I didn't remember that my friends, my brother, my daughter and parents were by my side for weeks with love and care, and often with fear when I didn't recognize them, that I cried in pain whenever I was moved or turned, or that my close friend, Brenda, slept in the hospital room for many nights, an alarm set, in order to insist that my pain medications be given to me during the night, so my mornings would be free of suffering. All this was forgotten, only to be told to me, in parts, later. It was a story that seemed to have happened to someone else. My memory was given me in the words of others. I ask my friends and family over and over again for them to tell the story still being told. It is a fine, fine art, that of forgetting in times of pain. But it is also frightening when my doctor asks me how was your Christmas and I can't pull up a single detail or memory.

Author Meridel Le Sueur wrote an apt description of memory, calling it the event that re-members the dismembered. I know this kind of remembering now in a new way.

Not only did my outward vision change, but now I see like a horse; a shadow on the ground is an object to step over, a streak of sunlight along the floor looks like a cliff with a drop-off; and over two years later, I have still not reached the bottom of forgetting and remembering.

Recently, on another ambulance ride, my third in the aftermath of this same injury, I asked the drivers what had happened to me, to see if they could offer testimony and witness to my accident. But the mystery remained; I was found on the road. Later I found out the name of the woman who called 911 and talked with her and wept about what had happened. I was on my back, she said, my leg bent behind me.

▲   ▲   ▲

FOR MONTHS LATER I sat at home in my one place on the couch like a spider in the center of a web, with books around me, an apple, a walker, crutches, a tool for reaching objects, and I looked out at the snow on the hills and on the trees, grateful to be alive, so grateful that my eyes filled with tears at every kind thing someone did for me. I buried my face in my hands and I wept. I couldn't stop. It was part of the brain injury. Some people become violent, some only laugh. I cried. And while some people say that crying carries a person to the future, it carried me on a current to the past, to each cold place that has ever hurt, and I cried like a child. About love that wasn't there, love that now is. I cried because I could look, really look, at people, could see their hearts, their lapses of love, their capacity for beauty or evil, and also their many kindnesses. I could see more clearly with my inner vision. I no longer minded crying in public. I knew I was fortunate, considering the other possibilities in an accident like this, but I knew also I would never be the same person I had been. There is no doubt about it, and this is every brain-injured person's story. And it seemed no one, none of us, could grasp this. I was changed. This would be my dismay, especially as my frightened daughter drifted away from the stranger she called her mother. I was another person, another self. But it would also be an awakening, a return of attention to this body, the poetry of the bone of my pelvis, hip, pubis. The way all those places of pleasure are now only pain and breaking. If I leaned an inch in the wrong direction I was reduced to crying. "Reduced," as if shrunk, as if cooked into something strong and articulate, while the real pain is so large, so much larger than the dilute walls of skin.

And, what I never reconciled, that I loved, still love, the thing that hurt me.

That day something dark came toward me. No one else saw it, or admitted that they did. The folks on that corner of the road are drinking buddies with one another, some of them drug users. None of them had the integrity to stop by or call, but my other neighbors showed support, bringing offerings from the heart, food, a little refrigerator I kept in my spider's corner, a container of buffalo bone soup.

▲   ▲   ▲

ONE OF MY friends later heard the young man at the post office still trying to sell Big Red Horse, saying the horse had never thrown anyone. He was "a gentle horse, a family horse." He could have been right. I'll never know. The horse later vanished. The girlfriend said it had thrown three other people. The man said I was stupid. Once, a year later, he hid his face behind his mail and laughed when he saw me as if he was nothing more than a mischievous child who had played a prank on someone.

And the owner, the one who had traded the horse for a man, left town with our postmaster. After the accident she left town for nine months. Later, their relationship over, this man came by to tell me she had taken him to Aspen for a $4,000 weekend while I was in the hospital not recognizing my own family, my stomach black-and-blue from shots of blood-thinners. And then a year later I watched as she bought a $250,000 house for her daughter, tore it all down, and built a new one, starting from scratch, building along with it an anger in me I'd never known before. My loss, no consequences for those involved in it.

▲   ▲   ▲

THERE WERE NO witnesses to my accident. No willing ones, that is. I have only shards of memory, remembering only the inability to change anything in that slow movement toward possible death, and the story of the woman who found my body in the road. From the kind of injuries, it seems I was dragged, head on the ground. All I can say now, again, is that something dark came toward me and that horse. After sleep, after amnesia, after inhabiting different worlds, I no longer know what truth there is in memory. I believe things I didn't believe before. About what is outside us. About what is inside. It is a new geography, that of the forgetting body and mind, the remembering spirit, a new landscape. If in the brain, connections are sheared away, there is no way to lay claim to a strand of memory, a story, a moment in human time. There is no place named for this realm of unremembering. Finding oneself here is devastating, though there are at times fragments of beauty.

World Beneath

AFTER LIVING ON earth, I was, for those weeks, beneath it, in a darkness and unknown that might have been a little like death, a feel for the unstoppable future. But I was not afraid of the dark. Underneath, there was grace. I saw beautiful things unseen by everyone else around me. Where others looked out and saw a brick hospital wall, I described to them a Chinese museum through the glass outside my window, told in detail of the silks, embroideries and carvings, the enamels and jades that, in my life, I had never before seen. I saw a woman and her two children who had once been in the same hospital room. And I saw people I can only describe as sacred and beautiful, ancestors of mine, presences. There was the man of my tribe, in a red-and-black-striped shirt, dark hat, and a beautiful dancing woman who floated in air and wore a lavender dress. I reported to my friend that these people insisted I follow their ways. I was visiting, I think now, places few humans ever come back from.

Amnesia isn't just a mystery of the brain. It includes the human spirit. Even later, when others thought I was awake, I was in a forever unremembered state. I wonder who was it, the woman so completely honest and crying? The one who broke all the rules of social facade, and yet who also saw the realms of beauty, the Chinese room, the ancient people. Who was the woman weeping into her parents' laps, the one who traveled to other worlds, the worlds where dream and waking reversed in the mysterious labyrinth of the brain, never again to be reflected on.

I had come apart, but in that breaking was a ray of light; it was the soul that remained. To lose memory and time throws the idea of the self into doubt. I can only think we humans consist of a unity of selves, a juncture.

It is a mystery and also a place of intersections, like where the two roads meet, where the red horse lived.

It wasn't that I entered the world of death as my father once did when I was fifteen. He had a heart attack. He returned with a back-from-death story of light and peace. Ironically, after his later surgeries, this peaceful, beautiful place in death was forgotten. For me, I went somewhere other than death. Amnesia, a country of ghosts, a no-woman's-land. There, the daily details of a life no longer count. It is a place of secrets the self keeps from the self.

There, there was no longitude or latitude, no named location. It was a secret island. It was a place where people spoke to me, where they were beautiful with strong words. I wasn't afraid, though I often asked if I was going to die or if I'd been in a car accident, as if I couldn't comprehend what had happened to me. Of my time in the hospital, my friends say I mostly cried with compassion about the other people in the head trauma hospital, grieving their losses, their comas, their paralysis, all of it making me seem nearly uninjured. But that was before I knew how deep a brain injury can go, how long the trauma lasts, and how I'd forgotten the entire hospitalization in that place. It was not like dreaming. As thinker and writer Laurens van der Post said, I thought I "was bonded to a greater, indescribable memory." And I knew that there, in that mystery, a human is a million years old and that what we call self extends beyond skin. The human is a country and the country is more than a human, than one person's world. Who was it within me, I ask now, that was connected to the universe and saw beauty unlike any I'd seen before, outside a window that held a view of only bricks?

Writer Donella Meadows says, "There's a part of me—it feels as if it is buried deep—that shines. It literally shines, or so it seems to me, with a warm and steady glow." That part, she writes, seems simultaneously inside and beyond her, connected to the universe. Perhaps that part was where I lived and where I forgot this residence.

▲   ▲   ▲

TO LOSE MEMORY and time throws the idea of the self into doubt. It splits apart all the notions of psychology. We humans consist of a unity of selves, the body a juncture, a union where the two roads meet. I had come apart, but in that breaking was a ray of light; it was the soul that remained. There would follow a series of awakenings.

I knew, in those hospital visions, who I was, even though I was no longer the person I had been. I would never be. I was returning to the Indian world and my own ways. There was yet a central core that remained, somehow undamaged. A year later, unable to teach, I'd be living in a different house, with a different dog, a new job working for my own tribe, owning two horses, one of which is Mystery, the wild mustang, the other a rescued horse, Kelli, who'd been wounded and was severely underweight.

Kelli

IN THE HOSPITAL I thought of horses. Instead of my moving away from horses, the accident made them more strongly in my mind. It was all I thought of.

Months later, as I was beginning to walk, the phone rang

one day and it was Colorado Horse Rescue. They said they thought they had a horse for me. There were two hundred people on their list and it was an average of a two-year wait, and I'd given up long ago. Would I come to see her? Still on two crutches, I went out, over the plains and past the railroad tracks. There were many horses, some so thin and starved they could barely move or lift a head. Some were injured and old. Many were saved from the horse killers. Now they were well cared for, and Kelli was in a small pen by the barn. She was so quiet, not even looking at us, as if she had no further hope. She had given up. The owners dropped her off and left her, an act that always surprises me, because my own commitments and promises are lasting. An Arab and Welsh mix, she had an off-center white blaze down her face. She was a companion horse. They had judged her unable to be ridden. The riders at the horse rescue said perhaps she was stubborn, but more than likely she was hurt. The owners had been running and jumping this twenty-year-old, and one day she rolled and she never ran again. She couldn't run, they said. She had papers, but they didn't tell me that, because they worry people will take horses only for their papers. There is a great corruption around horses and money.

Kelli had signs of many saddle sores and other wounds, and was seriously underweight. Later I would find that her hooves had been badly bruised, with blood still red in them. Her face also looked injured, a darkness around the cheek. She was unable to run, and she was a tragic-looking little mare. I was happy to have her as a nonridable companion horse. It gladdened my heart to think I could look out my window and see her.

In order to have her come to be with me, I had to prove myself worthy. I had to know the best of food, how much, what problems might be there, and I had to take her on a walk, not an easy task on crutches, but I undertook it anyway. One of my crutches fell as she pulled to the right as if to leave me, and she stopped, looked at the crutch, looked at me, and came back to walk at my side. She would prove to be my companion.

Later, in a herd, she became my guardian. If two horses kicked at each other, she came between me and them. When once all the horses ran into an arena by accident and I called Mystery to come out, Kelli went in and cut her from the herd and brought her out to me.

We healed each other, in a way. While still on crutches, I went to the farm nearly every day. It became a ritual. I breathed the good air, walked Kelli to fresh pasture. I brushed her mane and cleaned her coat. She gained 250 pounds and began to shine, and one day I came out to the farm and she was running. What beauty, a horse running, tail high, head back, mane flying. "I thought she couldn't run," I said to a friend. Looking at her, my newfound friend, Lori, said, "The problem wasn't Kelli, it was the people who had her." The vet later seconded the opinion. She was ridable.

Soon I was no longer on crutches. I wasn't healed in the brain, but my heart and soul were coming along at a quick pace, as if I too was running, just not over a curve or bend of earth. Time passed, and in it was a series of wakings.

Waking

I WOULD BE constantly waking up, asking myself over and over who I was, what I had been, where I would now go, what would I, could I, do. I was simultaneously bereft of my former self and given over to my new creation, as one doctor said, rewriting a self from the molecular interior of the brain. There would follow a series of wakings. I'd wake to find myself in the grocery store, with nothing I could remember I needed. I'd walk from room to room in my home. "Finding myself" is an apt term for it. One day I found myself on the ground of the creek, hysterical, weeping until an ambulance was called for me. It was thought at first to be a reaction to medication, but later, I knew it was because I had been hit with the realization that I was not healed as they told me I would be. It was around the time of my accident the previous year. Falling. That word was what my life had become in every way. One night when I was turning off the lamp, the room began to spin. Crawling to the phone, falling, once again I was unable to get up, again on the ground.

▲   ▲   ▲

ONE DAY AFTER my fractures healed, I woke with a lamb in my arms. I was sitting on the earth in mud, holding a sick lamb in a downpour of water. I smelled its stiff coat.

That day, after I'd spent time with Kelli, I'd heard a cry from the other side of the farm. It was Lori, calling, "Help." I went over and found her with a lamb that was bleeding at the belly and unable to walk. I called the vet and took the phone out to her, then carried the lamb toward the house, where I held it still. Soon another woman who kept her horse on the farm came and stood over us holding an umbrella in the rain. I let the lamb up. It seemed okay by then; it had gotten out and eaten too rich grass. The vet told Lori that the visit would cost at least eighty dollars, which was the market value of a lamb. "But I love it," said Lori. Sitting in the rain, I thought, I am fifty-two years old and my life is devastated and there is nothing else I would rather be doing than holding this little bleating creature whose mother, even then, kept an eye on me. Even the rain felt precious. I was again in the middle of life. But a different life.

On the Human Love of Horses

VICKIE HEARNE, WRITER, philosopher, and horse trainer, said, on working with horses, "While love is a dangerous guide, there are parts of the forest we sometimes find ourselves in that no other guide ever guesses the existence of." This is what I know. It was what moved me toward horses, entering that forest with its richness unguessed. I was from a world of horsemen, men who were in rodeos and drove cattle and had roping skills and rope tricks, like my dad. It took me half a century to enter it, this world that was in my DNA, this unguessed, unforeseen mystery, and I would never go back. Love truly was a dangerous guide, yet it led into that forest no one else, not even myself, could guess. Love.

My words to my friend that day were true; the red horse changed my life. For four weeks in the smooth sheets of a hospital bed, I worried about the horse, how he felt leaving me hurt behind him. I had compassion for the horse. Later, still on a walker, I had someone drive me by and we looked at each other, I felt him with my heart. One afternoon, I sat there with a friend in the car, discussing how heartbreaking this was for me. Big Red Horse looked at us. Then he straightened up and looked away, watching with excitement as another neighbor's horse, Chumly, came running up the road, white mane and tail flying. Chumly was greatly beautiful in his happiness to visit Big Red. They stood together at the fence like horses do. Then, one day, the red horse was gone. They "had to" to get rid of him, one neighbor said, then corrected himself and said they had sold him.

On animals, we believe they see our souls. We show them the best, the deepest, of ourselves, what we can't show other humans. Or sometimes we show them the worst, the most horrific, violent parts of ourselves which can't be shown to other humans. Vickie Hearne also said of us that "our words speak into the darkness to another creature."

Honesty

INJURED, I HAD an urgency for honest emotion, truth-telling, as if it was basic to a life, to our very existence. And I see now that it is. Truth is a form of freedom. Truth is a form of love. And love requires honesty. And so I asked of my family all the unasked questions of our lives.

My parents are of the generation of silences, while my generation is the generation of openness, wanting our memories and recollections. We come from different times. Later, unremembered by me, I asked the unaskable questions, broke through the silences of all the previously unspeakable things in our family. I entered the country of the past so the future would hold healing: Like Lot's unnamed wife, I looked back. It's what people do in hospitals so much of the time. Because of this fall, we did love and we grew, and again in those little moments of mishaps and pain kinfolk pass through, they turn once again into family, with a bond that was something more than just blood. And there is forgiveness all around.

I remember, out of the fog of the time, that my father had a dignity and honesty I will always admire. And my mother, I saw her as an innocent, with her fear of emotion and a hurt from unknown sources inside her, and I loved her for the offerings she had made to my life in the hardest of times, like the time she helped me escape a drunken man and the time when we couldn't afford it, but she sacrificed to buy a green dress for me for a school dance. They came to my house and did labor, my mother cleaning the kitchen until it was beautiful and shining, my father making the yard so neat that I'd want to sit outside.

And his smiling advice: "Never trust a man who tries to sell you a gentle horse." I laughed. Because it is true, gentle horses are usually not sold. I know now that horses are often drugged by sellers in order to make them seem gentle and easy. It's a business with a very small measure of ethics. My father is a cowboy. From days when the horse traders came through the west of Oklahoma, Texas, and the South. He is part of a rodeo family. His father a wild bronc rider, his brother a farrier and trainer, another a bull rider. He was once, when Indians were cowboys, a "breaker" or trainer.

Once I was home, in need of constant care, my brother, Larry, came to stay with me in the most heroic fashion, sleeping nearby on the floor, even though it made his work days longer, bringing me coffee at five in the morning before he left for the day, giving mouth-to-mouth to my dog that died on Christmas Day, just two days after I'd come home. When he wasn't there, my friends came to spend the night, my friend Brenda even flying in from Seattle to help. All of them, and my elderly parents, beautiful in their displays of love and care. And so I cried my way into a love that has become like muscles defined, strengthened. As if those lean parts are delineated in beautiful ways, as in a mighty horse.

That is the beauty of the brain, awe and admiration, the holy.

Our family changed. So did my life. I was no longer independent, and my own heart, that of an introvert, opened a bit further. The pain, the accident, transformed us all into something better as people, and finer than pain. It was a way of putting life together again. Not just the healing of the body but something more than that. As if harmony and balance, that name I had chosen for the horse, were the final destination, after all.

Whoever I'd become in the hospital, the woman unremembering and unremembered, wrote about how a single moment changes a life: *Always I know a life is only a moment from change, or a day, a week, a sperm or egg. Or that a breeze of love appears from the east one morning. A dog walks to your door with a thin belly and a hungry eye. A young person takes your hand and says, I will help you, as happened to me years ago in Mexico. The nectarines grow on the tree you planted from a seed one year and they are sweet.*

Maybe forgetting is as fine an art as remembering. It is what humans do when there is no understanding. To seek something of importance is one of our traits, as some of us are intent on understanding each incoherent part of life. But life itself is the unknown and in a split second it can change.

BONES, AND OTHER
PRECIOUS GEMS

His Father's Bones

IN THE EARLY 1900s, six living Eskimos were taken to the Museum of Natural History in New York for what was called a scientific study. One was a six-year-old boy named Minik; he accompanied his father, Qisuk, and four others. Their story was uncovered not long ago by an Iqaluit businessman, Kenn Harper. Harper had met Minik's mother in Greenland, and she told him the tragic story of those who had gone away. Harper wrote a book about it, *Give Me My Father's Bones*. In it he chronicled the lives of the Eskimos on the East Coast. In a *Washington Post* article in 1992, there was an early photograph of the infant Minik in his own land, on his mother's back, crying as if he knew what the future held. His mother was beautifully dressed in seal-fur clothing.

There was money to be made in native bodies, alive or dead. Robert Peary, the explorer and exploiter of the north, made a fortune from this live human exhibition. Franz Boas, the well-known anthropologist, was also involved.

At the museum in New York, Minik and his father were exhibited as curiosities and scientific specimens. They stood naked for scientists, anthropologists, photographers, and others whose work it was to compare races. Minik and his father lived in the museum basement amid bones and skulls, in an underworld beneath the New York summer heat, with the world of the city outside probably as frightening as that inside. Minik's father was frequently photographed in ridiculous, humiliating clothing, including golf socks "with a loud pattern." Minik, the boy, played with stuffed sled dogs that were part of the exhibition.

One day, according to Harper, a doctor, apparently studying the differences between colors of skin and how it healed, burned Minik with an iron. His father, by then sick with tuberculosis, got up from bed in order to fight the people who thought they owned them. Seeing his father so enraged, Minik lied about the source of the burns, saying he had done it himself. The next morning his father died. It surely must have been as much from heartache and sorrow as from tuberculosis.

▲ ▲ ▲

TIME PASSED. MINIK forgot his native language and events from his earlier life at home. Then, one day, years later, he went into the museum and found his father's skeleton on display. When he saw it, he said in his own words that he wanted to die "then and there." The view of his father's bones on display traumatized him for the rest of his life. In a ruse to appease and silence him, a funeral was faked, with the help of well-known anthropologist Boas. Another skeleton was buried.

The bones of Minik's father were taken apart and distributed elsewhere in the museum for later study.

Years later, Minik went home to the north. "Incredibly he relearned the language," Kenn Harper writes, and became a hunter. For a while, he was a guide and interpreter. Later, like many indigenous people who had no immunity from European diseases, he died from influenza.

It is significant that seeing his father's bones was what traumatized him the most. This need for ancestral bones is still significant. There is now an assembly of 700,000 First Nations people in Canada asking for the return of the bones of their mothers and fathers, grandmothers, and other ancestors.

The Marvelous Network

THE HUMAN BODY and its contents used to be considered sacred habitat. The body was mapped in many differing ways in different cultures and times. While most people now think of it as merely an architecture composed of living cells, bones, and calcium phosphate, at other times it was thought to be a beloved creation of mystery and awe.

The bodies of European saints were believed to contain viscera made of rubies, lapis, and other gems. The treasures inside the holy body were more precious than those of humble peasants or kings. They were preserved in cathedrals and catacombs and under glass.

Not only were the insides of bodies considered precious, but gems were also used to heal diseases. Nostradamus, with all his family dead from the plague, created healing potions made of ground pearls, gold, and lapis. And now the Japanese, in their recent lavish time, are drinking gold dust in their wine.

▲   ▲   ▲

KNOWLEDGE ABOUT THE body, at least in western thought, was slow to develop. There are reasons for this. In the European past the anatomy of the human body was described only in books. The human body was taught to medical students in words only. There were no visual representations. Leonardo da Vinci protested this flaw in medical education. He wrote in his notebook, "You who think to reveal the figure of man in words, with his limbs arranged in all their different attitudes, banish the idea from you, for the more minute your description the more you will confuse the mind of the reader and the more you will lead him away from the knowledge of the thing described . . . away from the love for such things." Away from love, I think, is significant, because with his own work Leonardo paid such a loving tribute to human flesh and muscle, and the light in a human eye.

▲   ▲   ▲

GALEN, ONE OF the fathers of western medicine who himself used this verbal description of the human body, was discovered, by one of his students, to be wrong. Vesalius, the student, looking for bones to study, began stealing the bodies of the dead. With luck, as he put it, he found a dried cadaver on the road. He thought it was probably a thief who'd been caught and killed and left to decay. The bones were bare, he said, probably cleaned by birds, and were held together only by the ligaments. He took them home and carried them secretly past the gate of the enclosed city.

In Vesalius's research, he found that Galen had fabricated much of human anatomy, and had based it on animal anatomy. Galen had described a "marvelous network at the base of the brain" which appears in animals, but not in humans. This marvelous network we humans are missing seems most interesting to me. I can't help but wonder what it is that we are missing.

Bones and Pearls

IN ANCIENT TIMES, the Southeastern tribal people I come from had a group of people called bone pickers. The bone pickers kept their fingernails long for removing the flesh of the dead. They had a special place within the fabric of the world, because the cleaned bones of the beloved dead were important to those who revered the bodies of their ancestors.

Hernando De Soto was one of the invaders who described the ways of the people I came from, but what I've remembered most strongly about De Soto is how he persuaded a woman from one of the Southeastern tribes to guide him and his men to another location in order to steal her pearl, the kind of pearl Nostradamus might have used to heal the sick. It was the largest he'd ever seen, and he desired it. But at night, while he slept, the woman stole back the pearl and disappeared into the darkness of the land she knew, leaving De Soto and his men lost and outraged over such poor behavior on her part.

In spite of his treatment of the native people, De Soto was one of those who related some customs of the Southeastern tribes, and his words and descriptions were historically significant. He wrote of ancestral bones kept in baskets and cared for by priests. He described temple mounds that contained the ancestral bones within. Later in history the customs changed. Some years later the humans were buried beneath their homes. Later, small houses were built over the gravesites of the buried, loved dead.

The veneration of body and bones is common to all humanity, not just the tribal. We have only to think of the Egyptians and their methods of preserving the bodies of their royalty. The calcium phosphate by which a person stands is the closest thing the body has to eternity. In that respect, the soul and the bones are not so different from each other; both are thought to be eternal, or nearly so.

Elephant Bones

THE CARE FOR bones is not only common to most of humanity, those without that marvelous network at the base of the brain, but to other species as well. Elephant researcher Cynthia Moss has written about how elephants care for the bones of their dead. "It is haunting and touching," she says. The elephants return to the bones, "sometimes lifting them and turning them with their feet and trunks." Traveling elephants, Moss observed, detour from their route in order to visit the bones of their dead. They returned and touched their kin time and again, resting against the skull bones of child or mother. The son of one matriarch remained behind, moving his mother's bones, placing his trunk mournfully on her skull and jaw each time he passed by. Another time, Moss chanced to see a burial ritual in which the elephants were putting earth on the body, going away and returning with palm fronds to cover it. They had begun to bury it in this poignant manner, with purpose, until they were interrupted by the plane that carried ivory-seekers.

Travels to the End of the World

IN OUR MORE recent times, there are ultrasounds, X-rays, and MRIs that reach into the human body to diagnose, but traditional healers know the terrain not only of a sick person but of many worlds. Seeing inside the body with a vision unknown to the rest of us, seeing and reading the bones, sorting through the anatomy, they determine the source of illness. Not in a careless manner as western doctors once did in the past when they operated on merely a kind of hope, cutting people open and unwittingly rearranging their organs without knowing what belonged where. Nor are traditional aboriginal healers spiritually careless, as are those who count on patients' belief and faith to heal them, such as a preacher who blamed a deaf girl I knew as a child for her own lack of healing because she "didn't have enough faith."

Evidence of many traditional healing methods is seen sometimes in ancient rock paintings where humans with bones were made visible. Also, there is evidence in some surviving written records: The Egyptians had medical knowledge of the circulation system over a thousand years before this knowledge was learned in western medicine. The Mayans also had medical knowledge, but it was burned by the Spanish, except for one or two collections. The hidden inside, as with art and love, is revealed in these cultures. The ancient ones had recorded it in their medical histories.

Many indigenous healers search the universe or the ocean

for a soul gone astray, or stolen. They travel across the threshold of body and skin to enter another world, because there are other journeys than inward ones. The sojourner may travel into the sky realms. The healer, like Jacob, climbs into the sky in search of the soul. Or to the underworld, or beneath the ocean to the Eskimo goddess Sedna, who lives in the sea. Or, as with the Cree and Anishnabe of Canada, a mountain of forty rivers and mineral medicines is visited and entered.

As with outward journeys, the journey to the bones, the organs, the interior, is one a healer or a sick person must take in order to seek a cure, as if following illness back to its origins and remembering the body history as a kind of map or story. Maria Sabina, the unfortunately exploited Mazatec healer, said, "I go along the path of the tracks of your palms, I go along the tracks of your feet. I am going there, I am arriving there." In the spirit world, as well as in the physical, healers follow and remake the human body.

For the Tlingit, there is the Master of Sickness, the Master of Pain. Perhaps that master still exists. Or the sea goddess who, when appealed to, will render powerless the things that harm. Or a path of pollen, as in Navajo ceremonials, to follow to a better way. In these times it seems easy to believe in an indifferent, lifeless world. But then we are indifferent toward it. As with all cases of soul loss.

Sometimes, in some traditions, the spirit of the ill is searched for and found and returned to the body. Sometimes, even with all the temptations to remain on earth, it is not. In old China it was the River God that was entreated, and so was the soul of the departing.

The River God is said to live in a fish-scale house in the water, and it is there that the healer goes on a journey in order to retrieve the soul of a sick person whose life energy has wandered away. The healer searches the spirit world and makes a plea to the River God to summon the soul: "There is a man on earth below who I would help. His soul has left him." Then he speaks to the departing: "Oh, Soul," says the God's helper, "why have you gone to the four far corners of the earth? In the east you cannot abide. There are giants there a thousand fathoms tall. In the south you cannot stay. There the people have tattooed faces and blackened teeth. They sacrifice the flesh of men and pound their bones to paste." And to the west, it's said, there are shifting, moving sands and empty deserts, red ants huge as elephants, wasps as big as gourds. In the north, says the God's helper, the ice rises high, and there are wolves and jackals. "Come back, Soul, come back to the gate of the city," says the healer. And then he tells the soul all that awaits its return. He tells what makes the world desirable. There are silks and balconies, views of the high mountains, good air, pearls and precious stones, vermilion, and a pool with lotus blossoms. All the beauties and comforts of the world are spoken in order to tempt back the soul of a dying person.

▲   ▲   ▲

FOR MOST OF us our journeys are not quite so large. We travel over the boundaries of suffering, illness, and war because there is no choice. Too often there is no one to call us back, to take away the illness, or to reassemble us. Our bodies are passing through life, following tracks of a different order from our desires and wills. And, too, the soul is still sometimes lost today. Perhaps in smaller ways than death, we lose the soul, a piece at a time, as when we turn away from what needs our help, remain silent when words are necessary, or take something from the world that can't be replaced—a plant, an animal, a love.

▲   ▲   ▲

IN ANY CASE, we are still searching out the causes of illness. We are sometimes hopeless, at other times hopeful. We are always seeking the reasons for our physical disasters. Nowadays it isn't just the breaking of taboo, but the wrong food, the placement of stars. Humans are always looking for aid from above, below, or around us, and even without believing, it is God, or one of them, at least, we call on when hurt, frightened, or in pain.

The Dress of Muscle and Flesh

ONE SEPTEMBER, YEARS ago, stopped in our truck on an Oklahoma highway, witnessing the results of a traffic accident, my father told me about his first heart attack. He said he had died for a while and gone to a beautiful place of light. He wanted me not to grieve too much when he dies again because it was the happiest he'd been in all his life. We laughed at the absurdity of death being the best experience of a life.

Then, over thirty years later, after open-heart surgery, he forgot this memory. What an irony, to forget such peace about death as it grows closer.

The spiritual country of the human is a sensed world, not a known one. It's a world where, put into words, meaning vanishes. Once grasped, it often disappears, like my father's memory about death and life. Disappearing with it are the comfort and lack of fear such a memory holds. Life is always sliding away or through us. Dr. Albert Szent-Gyorgyi, in his Nobel speech, said he'd always searched for the knowledge of what life is, "yet when I got there, I saw that the wonder of life had somehow slipped through my fingers along the way."

For myself, I have tried to dwell in the bones, as in a dream I had long ago, at the beginning of an illness, when I dreamed my own spine coming to life, green as the first rising of spring, alive and supple. Sometimes I see the dress of muscle and flesh worn by these bones, and wonder why I can't heal myself, why I can't change the body clothing as some believe, and let the bones be free, why I can't journey into the matter of my own body and touch the organs, loosen the ligaments where they hold things together, like the body Vesalius found, the network, the tangle not existing at the base of this human brain that sets us apart from animals who have so much grace. But the interior, the vital force, slips through all our hands, even with our own bodies.

Still, there is always hope, a greatness inside, as if a person could summon up the one right thing, the one right thought or word that would change or heal. It may be along the path of pollen the person follows, like at my home after the early morning rain washes the trees and the ground turns gold with the yellow dust of pine trees. Or beneath the sea where a person does not, cannot, return to silks, lotus blossoms, and views of the high mountains.

Emergences

AND THEN THERE is the journey of emergence, the open infant's head, the first glimpse of a new life, the shoulder, the first sight of a hand. My daughter's son was born by the knife and not through the body canal that brings most of us into the world. I watched and held her hand and talked with her. Her husband was standing at her head so as not to see the operation that took place in bright light beneath blue cotton sheeting. I watched, but I turned away when I saw the beginning cut, so long and curved below the large, child-holding belly, but not before I saw the blood beginning to draw itself to the world from within, to the other side of skin. The flesh was lifted with none of the holy regard and love I felt for her body; it was pulled away, tugged at by the doctors, who chatted with one another in the presence of the sacred. Some of my daughter's organs, like those of saints were thought to be, truly seemed made of precious gems, garnets, rubies, lapis, and pearl. As some of her organs were placed upon her middle, I thought how medicine is still a form of violence, and yet we hardly know or remember another way. *This is the place where stolen bodies have brought us*, I was thinking. *But this is what we have.*

Standing there, I felt triumphant that another Indian child was entering the world. I had recently been on the Saginaw reservation where 108 bodies had just been returned from museums and reburied. It was morning. I stood on the mound, seeing where the bones had been laid, at long last, to rest. We are getting back our precious gems, lives, bones, bodies.

And then the child was lifted from all that vulnerable alive, wet, and coiling matter. *My God*, I said, *he is so big.* Forgetting, a moment, in the joy of birth, my daughter, so open, so able to disappear from life in one split second, like all of us, and my love for her so powerful, for her body, those glistening body parts, and there was Michael, the baby whose bones would grow long and lanky on mother's milk. My daughter's body, yes, it was made of precious gems.

PHANTOM WORLDS

Phantom Pain

BEFORE MY MATERNAL grandfather, Edward Bower, died of a bleeding ulcer, he took aspirin for pain. It was the cure of the day. As a child, when I visited him I was his "little nurse," unwittingly bringing to him in his bed or chair not a source of healing, but an installment of his death, two aspirins and a glass of milk. In those days, that was the cure for ulcers. In the end, he bled to death. Before he was hospitalized, he'd been with his brothers cutting and stacking hay. They may have been drinking, my grandmother said, when he began to bleed. My grandmother accused his brothers of killing my grandfather. I was a child and only heard words from my aunts, that the room looked like a butcher shop, that he no longer minded the needles in his feet, that this was how they knew it was the end, because the nuns said the feet are the most tender part of the body, and he no longer felt them.

▲   ▲   ▲

ON THE TENDER nature of feet, I think of Dorothea Lange's photograph of her own feet. They look especially vulnerable, deformed by childhood polio, from which she never recovered. In her photograph, they are bent and misshapen, with extra bumps, and with toes not in the right shape for movement. Most of her documentary photographs reveal other people's suffering, the isolation and loss embedded in the faces of hunger and poverty and age of the Great Depression. She had an unsparing eye, and she captured pain on the faces of the destitute of America, former slaves, the Japanese going to internment camps, the hungry and hopeless and sick, the "Damaged Child" of sharecroppers. And then, in all this, in only one photo there is the photograph of her feet, bent, painful, and frail.

Perhaps all her photos might be considered autobiographical. The faces of her subjects are perhaps a statement of her internal world. Her photographs of those with canes and crutches were certainly a form of self-study; she herself used a cane. Her own lameness, she said, gained her entrance into the world of other people's suffering. Lange said, "No one who hasn't lived the life of a semi-cripple knows how much that means."

The photos left behind are something of a ghost world still here to haunt us with our American past. But it is her photograph of the terrified horse that speaks most powerfully, not only of Lange's own time in history, but of ours, of the harshly destroyed land. White, seemingly abandoned, the horse races in fear over a world just plowed, a torn land, no vegetation left, no water, and no place to go in order to live. It runs over the turned soil that just a short while ago, only moments before, had been long grasses and prairie abundance. In this picture is a geography of hopelessness and torn earth. The horse knows and reveals the truth of broken land, the unbearable histories and geographies that are far from invisible. This, too, is one of the shapes of pain, fully muscled, with hoof, mane, and tail. Seeing what others do not.

When artists render up the truth of their lives and those of others, it is as if they are cartographers introducing us to foreign worlds. Even with that, the world of pain is a place unreadable by many. Sometimes it is the pain of the earth, not of any one individual. Pain, also, as a friend once said, has the shortest memory. I say it runs like a terrified horse, with shock and fear of the phantom terrain.

▲　　　▲　　　▲

DURING THE TIME documented by Dorothea Lange, my family in Oklahoma was watching the world turn to dust. It was carried by winds away from earth. They lived beneath a sky made of sand. It had blown and sifted and laid itself down on tables, beds, floors, and sleeping children. The fine-grained world entered houses as if there were no doors, sifted against barns.

In this world my father and my Chickasaw uncles grew to manhood. My uncle Wesley was nicknamed Rip, both for his rodeo skills and, I suppose, for his recklessness, and the sure results both would bring about. Like my father, he went into the Civilian Conservation Corps and built part of America. Then, in the fifties, at the time when Indian people were being relocated to cities by government decree, he moved from Oklahoma to Denver, where he helped found an organization that gave assistance to the Indian people who were being bused into cities far from their homes.

One day, quail hunting, my uncle accidentally shot himself in the foot and lost a toe to the injury. I remember how he and my father would sit in Wes's overly clean house on the plastic-covered sofa near the fishbowl of guppies and talk about it as "the damnedest thing." Wesley's absent toe throbbed and hurt, and when it was stepped on or stubbed against the foot of a chair or bed, he felt it. The unevidenced fact of pain in the empty space inside his cowboy boot confounded him.

"Phantom" is the word for this kind of pain. Like other kinds of pain, phantom pain is a phenomenon known but not understood by medical professionals. Unlike other types of pain, no body part need be present for it to occur. Felt by amputees, it is an apparition, a ghost thought to exist only in the mind, as a memory unforgotten. But then, the problem with pain altogether is its invisibility. Maybe most pain is phantom pain, especially chronic pain. Subjective and suffered in a world and time of objective medicine, its existence does not always rely on a light spot, a shadow on an X-ray, or the frank evidence of blood. It belongs to the world hidden inside a boot, to secret histories of inner worlds, to beds where the sick are unseen, beds where human mystery, wounding, and love occur.

Pain is too often thought to be imagined, even in a world that usually believes in the hidden and invisible; God, angels, and atoms. This is a culture in which the soul is often still more important than flesh, pain is too often disregarded.

With phantom pain, what is yet unseen and unmeasured by the naked human eye is revealed by Kirlian photography which measures the light and energy around the human body. There is light in a place where the body part has been. The body is ordered in such a way as to remember itself, its matter, its leg or foot or toe. Only a light remains, and it is a mystery.

Phantom Worlds

PHANTOM PAIN HAS other incarnations than that of the human body. Not only are there interior places in a person that may hurt, untoward inner geographies, but in history and mythology there have been worlds, documented and believed in, that were never there. It is ironic that pain in the human body can seem so unreal, so invisible, showing itself only in breaks, swellings, tumors, or burns, while in history people believed in something as abstract as worlds that didn't exist. These worlds, and imagined continents, with all their false flora and fauna, were even documented on European maps. It's as if it is easier to believe the human body tells lies but maps, books, and words do not.

When the explorers and invading Europeans came to America by water, they did not know where they were bound. Their journeys were both risky and whimsical. Irresponsible sailors, they based their travels on no realistic maps. They had come a ways from the days when, on their boats, they released birds from cages and followed them home to land, but more often than not, it was fiction they traveled. They shaped their lives, and the world, by believing that their imagined world was God's map, true and clear and destined. Early maps reveal their fantasy. What was believed to live in water was drawn on these first maps, horned serpents and sea monsters they would later destroy, strangely shaped whales that looked little like the true animal that could die such an enormous, bloody, painful death.

In the great misunderstandings and curious inversions of outer and inner worlds were imaginary places. In their minds were fantasies of healing and riches, gold and jewels, malingering islands, rare sightings, and downright lies. The Spanish said that in this land the Indians had floors of silver and buildings of gold.

Phantom worlds have shown up on atlases, sometimes lingering for hundreds of years after the region had been surveyed, navigated, and charted. California was falsely recorded as an island, and even after it was known to be part of the mainland, it took two hundred years for the maps to be changed. You would almost think it is the human preference to believe in what doesn't exist and to dispute, even damn, what does.

It seems so human to be this turned around, believing in worlds that never were, many of them measured out and mapped.

▲   ▲   ▲

IN THE ATLANTIC, the ocean I had crossed as a girl so many years before, was an island called the Isle of the Demons. Talked about for hundreds of years, this island elicited great fear in voyagers. The screaming sounds given off from the island could be heard long before the island came into view. Thus its name. It was the place of a great winged and feathered mass of birds. The clamorous, deafening sounds they made were as mighty and massive as their populations. The air above was filled with wings, beaks, and eyes of birds. Drifting and falling feathers landed in water and were carried under by tides. The great auk, now extinct, was one of the species of birds that dwelt in enormous numbers on this island, off Greenland.

As the story of Demon Island goes, it was on this island a girl named Marguerite was put ashore and left behind for her love affair with a crew member, according to Don Johnson's book *Phantom Islands of the Pacific*. While in reality the island was populated by "swan white" polar bears, three of which Marguerite had to kill, the story of this pregnant girl was changed and transformed by the European imagination to better fit what was more commonly known of the world. Even though it was a place of glacial ice, the polar bears of the north, previously unseen by the Europeans, were changed by storied accounts into elephants and lions to fit the European imagination.

Maybe such stories were born of human need and desire, as Don Johnson suggests in his book. Or maybe they justified plunder and violence. Whichever, in history, stories were changed to accommodate what was familiar, sensational, or desired, as in a monk's story of "a long sea voyage in search of a blissful Otherworld."

It was the story that counted, with its fragments of knowledge and myth, as in the journey of Sinbad, or in Homer's *Odyssey* with its whirlpools, labyrinths, and creatures of terrible distinction, women seductive and wise, with beautiful voices and songful spirits.

In human journeys to unknown worlds, names were given, stories told, maps made, directions stated by men who were sometimes young, sometimes crazy, and almost always believed. Later there would be fictional narratives of captivity, white women stolen by Indians, a kind of fiction that developed on this continent. The truth was that often, once they were in the camps of Indian tribes, the Europeans wanted to stay.

The world has been brought to language, charts, and units of measure in many ways. It has been made and remade, sometimes diminished, sometimes extravagant. It isn't at all unusual for fragments of stories, myth, and only a glimmering of knowledge to contribute to great losses such as those of the auks and gannets on the Isle of the Demons. Worlds are made of lies and dreams. There were tales told in a drunken evening, words exchanged from a passing ship, and even a mere belief in something poorly glimpsed or felt.

Phantom Medicine

IT IS IRONIC and tragic that many books and records of medicine were burned by the Spanish. They may have been books that could help us now, in this time when medicine is returning for a look at plants and minerals.

According to philosopher Jacob Needleman, Mayan medical knowledge astonished investigators with its intelligence, as did an Egyptian papyrus from 2500 B.C., with its diagrams and knowledge of the circulatory system, which was unknown in the European world until the seventeenth century.

In the Mayan papers *The Chumayel*, the tragedy of history after the Spanish arrived is written into the conclusion. In the past, it says, before the Spanish arrived, things were good. "Whole the moon, whole the year, whole the day, whole the night, whole the breath when it moved, whole the blood, too." The book recorded the changes, saying that there had been no sickness, "they had no aching bones, they had no high fever, they had no smallpox, they had no burning chest, they had no bellyache, they had no chest disease, they had no headache until the foreigners arrived." Then "no good days were shown to us, no more sound reason."

Before and After

THIS PLACE THAT even Columbus called a paradise is even more quickly now becoming the place where Dorothea Lange's white horse, terrified, runs back and forth, seeing the destruction, the torn land. As if it remembered history, and history remembers the future.

▲   ▲   ▲

THERE IS ALWAYS, to everything, a before and after. "Before and after" is not just true with history or the Mayan *Chumayel*, but these are words spoken frequently by the injured, wounded, or ill. As an American Indian, I think of this daily, watching the continued destruction of land. I remember one day with the injured eagles where I used to work. It was a windy day, with gusts and blowing sand. When I went into their flight cage, the eagles were sitting on their perches or on the earth. As the wind blew, they closed their eyes and stretched their wings wide, the feathers overlying one another. And so it was that the eagles, when the wind blew, would remember wholeness and flight, and would lift their wings and close the gray membrane over their eyes, feeling it, their feathers touched and moved. Some of them, with their great wingspans, with the wings wide open and spread, would levitate slightly, as if in flight, softening. I knew what they were feeling, the phantom memory, the remembered life of before.

It is also what we Native peoples think, of the past which held us up. *Before*. Last month my tribe had a special calling, for people to go home. I was in Oklahoma already, and with my friend I decided to go to the Chickasaw Stomp Dance. I could leave early Saturday morning and head south. It was extremely hot. Temperatures reached as high as 108. When we arrived, a few people were moving about. I thought others would arrive later. With only a few families there, we decided to go into town and eat, get a room, then return at dark.

That night, because the dance begins late, we returned, but no one was there. The hills were empty.

The dance grounds were on a hill overlooking a valley. There was the place where the fire had been. I heard the songs, as if they lived in the ground. *Oh he ye. Oh he ye.* There were footmarks of the dancers who had been there the night before. It was silent. We looked at the footprints. Here is an Adidas, my friend said, and it made me laugh, the strange combination of cultures.

We sat in the darkness overlooking the red hills and trees, and my friend told about how years ago she wanted to go to the Hopi Snake Dance, because she wanted to know about people who honored snakes. It was a long drive. She drove for hours. When finally she arrived, the snake dance was just over, the snakes had been returned to their age-old dens, and people were shaking out dust from their blankets and clothing. She was disappointed to have arrived too late. She asked one Hopi woman if the dancers would be back, voicing her disappointment. The woman invited her in for dinner and said, Oh you arrived just in time. This is the best part. Afterwards, when everything is in balance and quiet.

Afterwards, even now, I feel the air as if I could move through it with my ancestors' wings.

Beginnings and Returns

NOT ONLY ARE there before and after, but there are also beginnings and returns. Not only is there the creation of the humans, formed of corn or clay, with a breath of wind or a god, but there are mythic destinies. Sometimes myth is formed by the body and what happens to it, especially in the realm of pain, death, and birth. Phantoms of generations past are in our bodies. These explain us to ourselves.

Each tribe has its own emergence story. In the Grand Canyon at a confluence of two rivers, up above the Colorado just a bit, exists a place of human emergence, one called Sipapuna by the Hopi. It, the center of their beginning, is an earth navel. While passing through on a journey down the Colorado River in the Grand Canyon, I went to that spot and swam in the red-brown rush of water from which it is said that humans emerged. The current grabbed me. Sand in my teeth, I was blinded by the silt and carried by the force of water. Forced sideways in the muddy water, breathless, dirty, finally I washed up to the shore, as if it was the shore of being human.

There are always beginnings and centers to the world. The human people emerge, or are shaped as clay. On ladders, with a stalk or reed, arriving into the present, the center, the road of emergence. And then, once there, the body's purpose is to use life up, to burn, to rise like clouds, to be left behind, to drown or sink or lie down in the woods at last. There are numerous stories of how humans escaped the misery of one world and climbed into another. There is the Tewa Pueblo first man who came from beneath a lake to the surface world. He was injured and then healed by the animals, and so, recognizing their grace and powers, he gained acceptance and was able to bring

204 ▲ LINDA HOGAN

up the other people from beneath the blue lake. When the people came up to earth, crawled out of a cave, or came from the garden of Eden, these are all beginnings. And yet in all the miraculous and profound creation, a world awesome in its beauty, myth, and mystery, with the people who rose from lakes or washed up onto riverbanks, it is at the threshold where change happens. Unlike phantom islands and malingering worlds, our stories and myths remain because skin isn't where a person ends. We live not only inside a body but within a story as well, and our story resides in the land as sure as the vision of Dorothea Lange's desperate, running horse.

Dark Matters and Light

THE LOSS OF species, as with the great auk on Demon Island, is also a sort of phantom pain. We feel it, long for them, without even knowing what it is that we feel and yearn toward. We try to replace what is lost with possessions, with belief, with false hope. Longing, as poet Ernesto Cardenal said, for something beyond what we want.

For the vanished, the space in which they lived is an empty space, a dark hole collapsing in our world. And those who sign away and violate their lives do not even know them, do not know what it is they are losing, the empty place, the lives lost from the world. They only feel it in a wordless place inside a man, or in the aching heart of a woman.

In my own life, I was changed by pain, shaped by history, transformed by events, viruses, accidents, even chemistries. But somehow, even through it all, there was something I managed to love into life. It wasn't grace so much as it was the courage to look at myself and others, full in the face with a core of honesty, to look upon a greater world. In my early life, I, too, was a collapsing star, and a black hole is said to collapse forever. Hopeless, I did not ever think I would, one day, be at any place of emergence, washed up like a first person from Sipapuna, nearly new in the world. But sometimes a person climbs out, against all odds, like the river dolphins of the Amazon who are seen to emerge from dangerous, fast-moving whirlpools.

This is what can happen to a human spirit and her body within time. Sometimes she passes through, unbidden, uncalled. At other times she is beckoned by a shred of bark, in a forest or a tendril of light, a flimsy tentacle, or fin in water, a story well told, a world divined from the calls of birds or moving water. It might be, this place of ours, as soft as where a breeze sometimes meets earth. It might be as harsh as when fire enters sea.

There is a place where the human enters dream and myth, and becomes a part of it, or maybe it is the other way around, when the story grows from the body and spirit of humankind. In any case, we are a story, each of us, a bundle of stories, some as false as phantom islands but believed in nevertheless. Some might be true.

Others might call us a destiny of wonders. When the sun falls on the arm, it is touched. Then she, you, I, may travel beyond human construction and invention. Even knowing that the horrible and beautiful are together in the world, we pass the threshold into something finer.

Whichever way a person goes, we only know it is not possible to stay in place, not in the horizontal layers of earth, not in the vertical world of people upright and straight. This is the human condition, and for each of us, it is mythic as well as ordinary because we live by stories and they are not always only our own.

What is unknown within us comes to the shores of ourselves in many ways. Things we haven't dreamed wash up, exhausted, followed by mythic means, a journey, or even just an ordinary morning become something else.

We are, in part, the body of earth. It might be that this place of ours is alive and radiant with the dreams of humankind as well as the power of, the motion of, air on a feathered wing as the eagles remembered flight when the wind blew.

Pollen

ONE MORNING, HERE at my place, after a rain, when the pines were washed, I stepped outside and it smelled of the trees. The entire ground was gold with their pollen, looking as if it was the gold the Spanish imagined. I thought, yes, there is life all around. It is not so far away. It is close to us. It dwells in a moment of silence. When air touches skin, or you smell the fresh earth after a rain, then there is a moment of healing, of grace drawn to a point, a radiant, and a radiance.

Nowadays, it seems we are always trying to match the world to ourselves instead of ourselves to it, the way it truly is. Yet human smallness is only too apparent. In such great universes as ours, we should try to match ourselves to the outside world, the faith healer called river, or a clay woman, broken, who watches over the earth. There are those who journey to retrieve the souls of the ill, to restore the breath of the world, the great store of cloud forest, the medicines in mountains, and the blue eye of the sea that closes or opens. This, the range of a world.

When people come home after work, when the doors are locked, or the hay placed before the horses, or the deer draw near, or the cattle rest in the fields, and the plants gain an unwitnessed inch of growing, the stalagmites lengthen, the crystals of earth sharpen in dark unseen caves, where those who live in the ocean come up for air, or when those who live in air immerse themselves in water, would it be love we feel? When our beliefs settle down to sleep and the streetlights come on, if we said matter was holy, would we then love and be joyous?